Cambridge Elements ≡

Elements in Politics and Society in Southeast Asia
edited by
Edward Aspinall
Australian National University
Meredith L. Weiss
University at Albany, SUNY

VIETNAM

A Pathway from State Socialism

Thaveeporn Vasavakul
Governance Support Facility Initiatives

CAMBRIDGE
UNIVERSITY PRESS

CAMBRIDGE
UNIVERSITY PRESS

University Printing House, Cambridge CB2 8BS, United Kingdom

One Liberty Plaza, 20th Floor, New York, NY 10006, USA

477 Williamstown Road, Port Melbourne, VIC 3207, Australia

314–321, 3rd Floor, Plot 3, Splendor Forum, Jasola District Centre, New Delhi – 110025, India

79 Anson Road, #06–04/06, Singapore 079906

Cambridge University Press is part of the University of Cambridge.

It furthers the University's mission by disseminating knowledge in the pursuit of education, learning, and research at the highest international levels of excellence.

www.cambridge.org
Information on this title: www.cambridge.org/9781108459075
DOI: 10.1017/9781108608312

First published 2019

A catalogue record for this publication is available from the British Library.

ISBN 978-1-108-45907-5 Paperback
ISSN 2515-2998 (online)
ISSN 2515-298X (print)

Vietnam

A Pathway from State Socialism

Elements in Politics and Society in Southeast Asia

DOI: 10.1017/9781108608312
First published online: February 2019

Thaveeporn Vasavakul
Governance Support Facility Initiatives
Author for correspondence: t_vasavakul@gosfi.org

Abstract: This is a study of Vietnam's socialist transition and state transformation, generally known as *đổi mới*. It examines the drivers of socialist-regime change, the nature of the *đổi mới* state, and the basis of regime legitimacy in Vietnam. The Element argues that despite its "one-party rule" label, the party-state apparatus that channels said rule has become fragmented. State-building during the *đổi mới* period has involved negotiations and bargaining that redefine authority and power relations within the state apparatus. The party-state's accountability projects are designed to target the specific self-aggrandizing tendencies of the state apparatus, its policies, and the abuse of state power. At the leadership level, the patterns of resource allocation underlying the *đổi mới* growth model as well as the VCP's cadre rotation approach have accommodated central and sub-national state elites across sectors and levels, helping shore up the legitimacy of the *đổi mới* state in the eyes of the state elite. The combined factors of sustained economic growth, expansion of political space, accountability, and tolerance of small-scale public protests have been key in strengthening regime–society legitimization.

Keywords: Vietnam (Viet Nam), state socialism, doi moi (đổi mới), transition, state-building, state transformation, accountability, legitimacy

ISBNs: 9781108459075 (PB), 9781108608312 (OC)
ISSNs: 2515-2998 (online), 2515-298X (print)

Contents

1 Introduction

Đổi mới is Vietnam's[1] revolution from state socialism. Literally translated as "change," *đổi mới* was officially endorsed at the Sixth National Congress of the Vietnamese Communist Party (VCP) in December 1986. The Congress highlighted an urgent need for changes in thinking (*đổi mới tư duy*) and leadership style (*đổi mới phong cách lãnh đạo*). It endorsed the rethinking of the notion of "socialist transition" (*thời kỳ quá độ lên chủ nghĩa xã hội*), reviewing persistent bureaucratic bottlenecks, reducing stagnation and waste, placing practical reliance on the people, and measuring success through results (Đặng Phong, 2009b; 287–385). Official documents indicate that *đổi mới* is still ongoing (Đinh Thế Huynh et al., 2015).

That Vietnam's transition from state socialism has brought about positive economic and political results is undeniable. In the decade prior to 1998, Vietnam performed comparatively better than all other socialist transition economies except for China, reducing its total number of poverty cases by half (Van Arkadie & Mallon, 2003: 6). Measured in current US dollars, Vietnam doubled its *per capita* GDP from $413 in 2001 to $836 in 2007, and passed the $1,000 milestone of a middle-income country ahead of the target date set for it by the Socio-Economic Development Plan of 2006–2010 (World Bank, 2008: 3–4). Since 1986, Vietnam has embarked on regional and international integration: it became the Association of Southeast Asian Nations' seventh member in 1995 and re-established diplomatic relations with the United States, implemented a US–Vietnam Bilateral Trade Agreement in 2001, and joined the World Trade Organization (WTO) in 2007. Politically, Vietnam's one-party state has remained relatively stable throughout *đổi mới*. The VCP has confronted neither a major political challenge from within nor large-scale popular resistance like China's in 1989. That *đổi mới* has yielded considerable economic and political success is no exaggeration.

However, from a state-building perspective *đổi mới* has been inhibited by state ineffectiveness, bureaucratic corruption, and periodic public protest. The state apparatus has been ineffectual at formulating and implementing coherent policy, while state officials have indiscriminately used state offices for private gain. Small-scale protests have erupted in objection to land management, industrial labor relations, plunder of natural resources, environmental degradation, and Vietnam–China foreign and economic relations. Individual protests against the *đổi mới* state have also emerged. In 2017, a petitioner at the Office of the Central Complaint Handlings reportedly assaulted an official over the Office's inaction. Similarly in 2018, another citizen, barred from

---

[1] For consistency, the spelling Vietnam has been used in this Element rather than Viet Nam.

voicing grievances during a meet-the-public session, hurled a shoe at the Chair of the Ho Chi Minh City People's Council. Overall, though Vietnam has succeeded in transitioning away from a centrally planned economic system, its success in building a post–central-planning state has not kept pace with emerging governance challenges.

Indeed, records on Vietnam's state-building efforts reveal some peculiar phenomena. In the 1990s Vietnamese newspapers coined the adage "the emperor's edicts stop at the provincial gate" (*phép vua thua lệ tỉnh*) to highlight dysfunction within state hierarchies. Such dysfunction continued under Prime Minister Phan Văn Khải (1997–2006), who at one point lamented that even he did not have the power to appoint or dismiss ministers. Similarly, Vietnamese citizens deprecated public administration with the quip that "public administration is public misadministration" (*hành chính chính là hành dân*).[2] Recently, as the state arena itself has degenerated into a vast marketplace for corruption, the pejorative term "interest groups" (*nhóm lợi ích*) has been used for coalitions of vested interests with influential backing within the state structure. Such dispersal of state power and seeming breakdown of the state apparatus are especially peculiar given that Vietnam's one-party state under the leadership of the VCP is so frequently described as "authoritarian."

This Element examines the state's transformation during Vietnam's shift away from state socialism, specifically the transition's drivers and their impact on the socialist state, and the emergent *đổi mới* state's nature, accountability, and legitimacy. Focusing on the interrelationship between drivers and the nature of the state will enhance an understanding of the process of regime change and the political economy of change. Tracing accountability and legitimacy will shed light both on evolving state and societal relations and on conditions for political and ideological mobilization.

There are good reasons to focus on the state in Vietnam. Existing studies of *đổi mới* rarely maintain a systematic focus on the Vietnamese state, and when they do, the term "state" alternately indicates an institutional structure, an arena of contention, a set of interest group relations, and various components of government (Kerkvliet, 2001; Kerkvliet & Marr, 2004; Koh, 2006; Gainsborough, 2010; Thayer, 1994 and 2014). The lack of a consistent focus and definition is curious given that the notion "state" (*nhà nước*) is not new in Vietnam's political writings but has been used in such stock terms as "state apparatus" (*bộ máy nhà nước*), "state management" (*quản lý nhà nước*), and "state management agencies" (*cơ quan quản lý nhà nước*). Additionally,

---

[2] These observations are drawn from local newspapers; *Tuổi Trẻ, Thanh Niên, Lao Động, Đại Đoàn Kết*, and *Tiền Phong*, which in the 1990s were considered progressive.

regardless of the particular definition, practical concerns have also emerged over the effectiveness of the Vietnamese state. A series of studies from the Fulbright Economics Program based in Ho Chi Minh City, for example, attributes the ineffectiveness of the Vietnamese state to fragmentation and weak accountability (Vietnam Executive Leadership Program, 2012, 2013, and 2015). Adam Fforde and Lada Homutova (2017), in turn, highlight inefficiency in formal political institutions of Soviet origin, institutions through which the VCP still rules, as a factor hampering state effectiveness.

Bringing a focus on the state back into an analysis of Vietnam's path from state socialism, this Element looks at the state as a set of organizations with specific regulative, extractive, repressive, and ideological functions in varying relation with non-state actors. This definition is predicated on the assumption that states express the combined domination of classes and fractions of classes over the rest of their society at particular points in time although no state is reducible to domination by such actors (Therborn, 1978; Anderson, 1983).

Unpacking the transformation of Vietnam's socialist state under *đổi mới*, I examine three interrelated processes: transition from plan to market, state-building, and evolving accountability and legitimacy. In tracking the transition from plan to market, I identify key state socialist structures that developed prior to *đổi mới* as well as drivers for change and the change process. In discussing state-building, I examine the impact of transition on the structure of the state apparatus and its power, the redefinition of authority relations within the state structure, and the political economy of state policy. I situate the discussion of accountability within the context of the VCP and various government responses to emerging legitimacy challenges to the one-party state.

I argue that despite the label "one-party rule," the party-state apparatus that channels that rule has become fragmented thirty years after the launch of *đổi mới*. This fragmentation is a legacy of thriving commercialized interests at the provincial level during Vietnam's transition from plan to market in the 1980s. While provincial "fence-breaking" practices propelled a successful economic transition, they had the systemic effect of undermining the power of the central state. State-building that has followed has required negotiating to redefine authority relations within the state structure. The balancing of commercialized interests within the state apparatus has led to the institutionalization of a decentralized state apparatus. Vietnam's accountability projects have reflected attempts on the part of the VCP, successive governments, and even citizens to curb the specific self-aggrandizing tendencies of state agencies, state policies, and the use of state power in the context of decentralization and fragmentation. Economic success and political stability under the one-party state in the era of đổi mới have, to a considerable degree, been shaped by the interplay between fragmentation and accountability.

This Element's arguments and empirical discussion are in four sections, the first of which discusses the state socialist regime prior to đổi mới and the process of transition. The second focuses on the development of the đổi mới state apparatus and its political economy, and the third focuses on evolving accountability. The Element concludes in the fourth section by reflecting on Vietnam's đổi mới from a regime change perspective and scenarios for further change.

2 From State Socialism to Transition

Hồ Chí Minh declared the independence of the Democratic Republic of Vietnam (DRV) in 1945. The years that followed until 1975 were characterized by protracted military conflict with France and later with the United States. At the end of the war with France in 1954, the Geneva Conference mandated a temporary division of Vietnam at the seventeenth parallel pending a national election, but the United States' intervention in support of the Republic of Vietnam prolonged that temporary division until 1975 (Kahin, 1986).

The Vietnamese communist leadership north of the seventeenth parallel adopted core Marxist-Leninist principles for state-building: leadership by the Communist Party, democratic centralism, public ownership of the means of production, and central planning. Vietnam scholars have used various labels to capture the political and economic system that developed under the DRV north of the seventeenth parallel and was later imposed on the liberated Republic of Vietnam after 1975: "bureaucratic socialism" (Porter, 1993); "the DRV model" (Fforde & de Vylder, 1996); and a "centralized planning and bureaucratic subsidy mechanism" (cơ chế kế hoạch hóa tập trung quan liêu bao cấp) (Đặng Phong, 2009b). In this Element, I use the term "state socialism" to discuss the state and the socialist regime prior to đổi mới in order to highlight, on the one hand, the prominent role of the state under the leadership of a communist party in creating an egalitarian society by means of public control of the means of production coupled with economic planning and a social security system, and on the other, individual responses to incentives that system created (Kornai, 1992).

At the same time, Vietnam is unique in that state-building evolved there in the context of protracted military conflict, first with France (1946–1954) and later with the United States (1954–1975), Cambodia (1975–1989), and most recently the People's Republic of China (1979 and throughout the 1980s and 1990s). Including the years from 1956 to 1975 when the nation was divided in two. Prolonged military conflict and political division fostered a link between socialism and nationalism on the one hand and the regime's orientation toward the masses on the other. In this section, I first discuss key features of the socialist state and then examine the drivers for transition.

2.1 Key Features of the State Socialist Regime

Under the DRV-controlled northern area, the VCP, renamed the Vietnam Workers' Party (*Đảng Lao Động Việt Nam*) in 1951,[3] institutionalized state socialist political, economic, and social institutions under one-party rule. Politically, the Vietnam Workers' Party formulated party lines that served as the basis for state management, placed party and state personnel, and carried out socialist ideological education. It adopted democratic centralism as the main principle in decision making: decisions agreed upon by the majority had binding authority. In principle, the National Party Congress, the highest institution within the party structure, met regularly to approve party lines, amend party statutes, and elect members to the Central Committee. The war years from 1951 to 1975, however, saw only two national party congresses: the Second Congress in 1951 and the Third Congress in 1960. Between the party congresses, the Political Bureau, the Secretariat, the Central Committee, and Central Committee departments handled decision making. The Vietnam Workers' Party, through the 1959 Constitution, endorsed a structure of executive, legislative, and judicial institutions. The Council of Government was headed by the prime minister, whose decisions, in principle, ministries, state commissions, departments at the central level, and provincial-level administrative units carried out. The Constitution granted the National Assembly considerable authority, although in practice it served more as a symbol of national unity than a legislative, representative, or supervisory institution. Under the DRV, the judiciary system only had limited independence (Beresford, 1988). To link the communist party and society, the Party relied on mass organizations. At the core were the Vietnam General Confederation of Labor, the Women's Union, the Ho Chi Minh Communist Youth Union, and the National Peasants' Union, originally set up at the founding of the Indochinese Communist Party/Vietnamese Communist Party in 1930 (Huynh Kim Khanh, 1982). In the 1950s and 1960s, the Party supported the building of the Vietnam

---

[3] Founded in 1930 at a conference in Hong Kong, the communist party was named the Vietnamese Communist Party by Hồ Chí Minh before being renamed the Indochinese Communist Party (ICP) to reflect the Communist International's strategic concerns. After the August Revolution in 1945, the ICP dissolved itself to encourage participation in an anticolonial united front. The ICP/VCP was revived as the Vietnam Workers' Party in 1951 until 1976 when the name VCP was restored.

Fatherland Front (VFF) as a united front organization, and also set up wide-ranging professional, cultural, and religious associations. All these organizations had the dual function of implementing Party doctrine and communicating feedback from members to the Party. Under the DRV regime, the Party controlled other political institutions either by placing party members in leadership positions or through the VCP's corresponding committees. Party statutes placed the People's Army of Vietnam under the party's Central Military Party Committee (Thayer, 1994). Dang Phong and Beresford (1998) use the term "partification" to characterize communist control of other institutions.

Economically, the Vietnam Workers' Party institutionalized state socialist economic principles: state ownership of the means of production, central planning, and distribution of labor. Between the Second National Party Congress (1951) and the Third Congress (1960), the Party carried out land reform (White, 1981; Moise, 1983; Vickerman, 1986). The following Three-Year Plan (1958–1960) introduced "production cooperatives" to replace the family as a basic agricultural production unit. Land and all means of production were owned collectively, with five percent of cooperative land allocated to households as private plots. Income was distributed according to labor. The Three-Year Plan also transformed private enterprises engaged in trade and industries into mixed private–state entities. The Third National Party Congress (1960), following the socialist bloc's emphasis on socialist industrialization and the need for economic self-sufficiency, prioritized the development of heavy industry (Beresford 1989; Chử Văn Lâm, 1990).

In terms of economic mechanisms, the Party adopted centralized planning and administrative pricing. Given that Vietnam was an agrarian society, these mechanisms were applied mostly to the agricultural sector. The state invested in infrastructure and supplied means of production such as fertilizer and tools to cooperatives at lower than market prices. In return, cooperatives delivered agreed targets at below-market prices. Cooperative members were paid "work points" according to the amount of time expended on each task after state quotas had been met and collective funds set aside (White, 1985; Vasavakul, 1999a). This system was predicated on the assumption that surpluses from collectivized agriculture would serve as inputs for state-led industrialization (Truong Chinh, 1959; Fforde & Paine, 1987). Studies on the industrial sector in the DRV are sparse, but available literature suggests that central planners set targets for state-owned enterprises (SOEs) while supplying required inputs, increasingly with foreign assistance, for those targets. These SOEs were managed by central, provincial, and district-level state agencies generally known as "managing agencies" or *chủ quản* (Fforde & de Vylder, 1996; Vasavakul, 1999a).

In addition to political and economic institution-building, the Vietnam Workers' Party institutionalized an extensive system of public and social services, ranging from health care and education to infrastructure and public utilities. In rural areas, cooperatives were the key agencies responsible for delivering health care and education (Houtart & Lemercinier, 1984). Trade unions, acting on behalf of SOEs, distributed goods to workers, organized social and cultural activities, allocated housing, and guaranteed worker welfare (Chan & Norlund, 1999). Prior to the intensification of the war with the United States in the mid-1960s, the Vietnam Workers' Party had, to a large extent, put in place the key structures of Vietnam's state socialist political, economic, and social institutions.

Under state socialism, party and state political power depended upon their ability to control and allocate economic resources. The system's legitimacy also depended on growth and improved livelihoods. Central planning in the DRV, however, was not without its challenges. Agricultural cooperatives suffered from low state investment, low procurement prices, and inadequate compensation. As a result, cooperative members increasingly turned their attention to their personal 5% of cooperative land, which yielded some 60% of cooperative member incomes (White, 1985; Đặng Phong, 2009a). Industries also suffered due to the mechanics of central planning. To improve efficiency, planners set higher targets while lowering input and performance pay. In response, enterprises underreported capacity and performance to negotiate planned targets and increase their inputs. At the systemic level, central planning in the DRV gave rise to a practice of "asking-giving" (*xin cho*) between planners, managers, cooperative producers, and workers across sectors. This tacit resistance to central planning and the resulting "everyday negotiation and bargaining" developed within the socialist state structure itself (Vasavakul, 1999a).

That the system persisted without any official call for "*đổi mới*" derives from the unique features of the DRV regime. Politically, VCP leadership was cohesive. Despite internal party conflict, there was no purge of key party leaders. At its worst, internal conflict manifested in the 1960s in an internal debate known as "revisionism" and the defection of a top party member in the 1970s (Hoàng Văn Hoan, 1986; Bui Tin, 1995; Huy Đức, 2012). Economically, the DRV's "forced modernization" did not lead to forced rapid collectivization or a cataclysmic "Great Leap Forward" as in the Soviet Union or China. Assistance from the Soviet Bloc and China also took economic pressure off of rural cooperatives to deliver surpluses for industrialization efforts. Although the regime–society relationship had at times been strained prior to the American war, especially with peasants during the land reform period from

1953 to 1956 and with intellectuals from 1951 to 1958, the Party was able to mobilize various strata of the society during the war, when the socialist economic framework and state–peasant relations were also sustained through nationalism (Vasavakul, 1995 and 2000).

The path to *đổi mới* originated in the imposition of the expanded DRV model on a reunified Vietnam. The Fourth National Party Congress (1976) endorsed the large-scale socialist development model General Secretary Lê Duẩn advocated. The Second Five-Year Plan (1976–1980) accordingly expanded the socialist agricultural cooperative structure from the commune to the district level while setting up high targets to be achieved across sectors (Đặng Phong, 2009a: 25–7). The 1980 Constitution of the Socialist Republic of Vietnam (SRV) enshrined the socialist model of development and state-building patterned after the Soviet Bloc. It confirmed the leading economic role of the state and collective sector while endorsing centralized planning mechanisms and a foreign trade monopoly. Politically, the Constitution codified the development of a centralized state apparatus. It endorsed the State Council that acted simultaneously as the collective presidency and the standing body of the National Assembly and established a Council of Ministers to function as the collective leadership of the executive branch. These new institutions reflected VCP leaders' vision of a full-fledged, centralized socialist state for the reunified Vietnam.

The imperative for *đổi mới* resulted from a combination of domestic and international factors working simultaneously. In the newly liberated South, the VCP's collectivization of agriculture and its nationalization of industry and commerce met with vehement resistance (Duiker, 1989). Challenges to the regime also mounted as a result of international factors such as the United States embargo that led to shortages of industrial inputs, the diversion of resources to Vietnam's engagement in Cambodia, the end of Chinese aid by 1977, and reduced aid from the Soviet Bloc. From a structural perspective, systemic problems evident in both the North and the South before reunification had consequences. The South's total dependence on aid from the United States prior to the Saigon regime's collapse created a vacuum that necessitated the DRV's self-sufficient economy to produce a North-South transfer of resources that precipitated an economic crisis (Paine, 1988; Beresford, 1989). Ultimately, such numerous and diverse impairments to economic control in the reunified Vietnam compounded to undermine the VCP's legitimacy, prompting it to rethink its socialist development model.

2.2 Transition from Plan to Market

The transition from socialism in Vietnam is an exemplary case of socioeconomic and political forces playing a role in driving regime change, especially considering its beginnings, the agents of change, and the change strategy. While the Sixth National Party Congress of the VCP officially endorsed *đổi mới* in 1986, practices fitting that description had already been taking place by then. The transition experience also indicates that *đổi mới* has been neither a top-down process with changes initiated by particular leaders, nor a bottom-up experience driven by grassroots-level actors. Rather, it was the outcome of interactions among networks of commercialized interests from the central to the local level and across sectors within a decentralized state socialist structure. This experience shows that the transition away from central planning was a separate process from the institutionalization of a post–central-planning regime, and it should be noted that while endorsing *đổi mới,* the Sixth Party Congress did not elaborate a master plan for the process of institutionalization; measures to build institutions were discussed only by subsequent party congresses and further elaborated by subsequent governments.

2.2.1 Beginnings and Process

There are at least two historical periods that could be considered the onset of transition: 1966–1968, when Vinh Phuc Province, a province in the Red River Delta, experimented with a contract system in agriculture, and 1979–1989, when the VCP allowed production units to carry out both planned and unplanned activities simultaneously.

The 1966–1968 experiment, generally known as "household contracting" (*khoán hộ*), was credited to Kim Ngọc (1917–1979) who served as Party Secretary of Vinh Phuc province from 1959 to 1977. Kim Ngọc supported an alternative approach for reorganizing agricultural cooperatives based on three types of contract. Cooperatives could contract individuals, households, and groups to carry out work packages and could re-allocate collectivized land or other production materials to producers. There was no restriction on contract duration. This experiment, however, ended in 1968 after just two years when Trường Chinh, a Politburo member and party ideologue, criticized it as a case of undisciplined management potentially leading to privatization (Đặng Phong, 2009a). According to the former chairperson of a participating agricultural cooperative, the criticism did diminish the extent of the practice but did not completely end it. With Party Secretary Kim Ngọc's tacit consent, one cooperative continued to apply the household contract system discreetly (*làm chui*) (*Dân Việt,* September 15, 2017). Kim Ngọc's initiative was officially recognized in 2009 when he was posthumously granted the prestigious Hồ Chí Minh Prize. The VCP newspaper, upon reporting the commemoration of the 100th anniversary of Kim Ngọc's birth, called Kim Ngọc's approach representative of *đổi mới* (*Nhân dân Điện tử*, October 3, 2017).

The 1979–1989 experiment represents another landmark for transition. To address economic crises, the VCP re-prioritized Vietnam's economic development focuses and moved towards the decentralization of production activities. The Sixth Plenum of the Central Committee, in August 1979, passed two resolutions that promoted agricultural, consumer, and export production, a key departure from the traditional emphasis on heavy industry. The Plenum also encouraged the involvement of all economic sectors, including the state, collective, public-private, individual, and even capitalist sectors. The consumer goods industry and the provincial-level industrial enterprises would take the lead in delivering consumer and export goods based on inputs from the agricultural sector.

Following the deliberations of the Sixth Plenum of the Central Committee came a set of landmark frameworks that paved the way for Vietnam's transition away from central planning. In 1981, Directive 100 expanded output contracts (*khoán sản phẩm*) to both groups of farmers and individual farmers in agricultural cooperatives, effectively reviving family farming. That same year, Decision 25-CP institutionalized a three-plan system consisting of an official plan to deliver state targets, a second plan on horizontal connections among enterprises meant to address supply shortages, and a third plan based on the enterprise's own market efforts. From 1982 to 1985, the VCP supported experiments with price reform. In 1986, the Sixth National Party Congress of the VCP officially endorsed *đổi mới*. In 1987, the VCP further reduced differences between free-market and official prices, abolished rationing for select commodities, removed checkpoints for internal trade, and passed a liberal Foreign Investment Law. In 1988, Resolution 10 further de-collectivized agriculture, reducing the role of agricultural cooperatives and strengthening the household sector. In accord with the *đổi mới* spirit, the Council of Ministers in March 1988 issued two important documents to legalize the private economy and the family economy. Throughout the 1980s, the VCP also endorsed the liberalization of domestic and international trade. In 1989, the VCP abolished the two-tier price system, raised interest rates to realistic, positive levels, devalued the currency nearly to the market rate, relaxed foreign exchange and trade rules, and equalized tax rates across economic sectors (Beresford & Fforde, 1997; Đặng Phong, 2009a). The abolition of the two-price system, according to Adam Fforde and Stephan de Vylder in their path-breaking study (1996), marks the end of central planning.

The official frameworks the VCP enacted between 1979 and 1989 should not obscure the fact that most of these frameworks developed out of provincial-level "fence-breaking" experiments. Key provinces whose documented history of fence-breaking drove their contribution to the transition process include Hai Phong, Nam Dinh, Ho Chi Minh City, Con Dao-Vung Tau, Can Tho, An Giang, and Long An. Hai Phong, a northern Vietnamese city, took the lead in partially de-collectivizing agriculture in response to food shortages. Initial results at the commune level led to the replication of the practice at the district level with support from city party leadership. The Hai Phong experiment served as the basis for the formulation of Directive 100. An Giang, a Mekong Delta province, went further to return the means of production in the agricultural sector – land and production materials – to farmers. The An Giang practice contributed to the preparation of Resolution no. 10 de-collectivizing agriculture (Đặng Phong, 2009a).

Ho Chi Minh City, for its part, took the initiative to address central planning mechanisms in industry and trade in response to a shortage of production inputs and infrastructure investment. The City's SOEs "saved themselves" by cultivating horizontal connections, a practice not previously permitted, to acquire loans and foreign currency, purchase production supplies, and market their products. Similarly, Nam Dinh Province in the Red River Delta designed a tripartite arrangement between the Nam Dinh Weaving Factory, state import and export companies across provinces, and a Foreign Trade bank. State import and export companies borrowed from a Foreign Trade Bank to purchase production inputs for the Weaving Factory, which, in turn, delivered the outputs back to the import and export companies for overseas sale. Some provincial SOEs extended their geographical operation across provinces through a barter system while also diversifying their production into secondary product lines after having identified "market demand" elsewhere. The survival of these SOEs gave basis to the formulation of Decision 25-CP, which allowed SOEs to develop plans for state targets and plans for market exchange. Additionally, Ho Chi Minh City took the initiative to purchase rice at market price from Mekong Delta provinces in order to feed city dwellers. In the same vein, An Giang and Long An, two Mekong Delta provinces, even went so far as to replace compulsory purchasing and distribution with market-based trading of foods, farm products, materials, and consumer goods (Porter, 1993; Đặng Phong, 2009a).

All these provincial experiments are considered fence-breaking, as they involved bypassing both public ownership and central planning regulations barring privatization of the means of production, horizontal exchanges among SOEs, independent acquisition of foreign currency, access to bank loans without central permission, or the use of market prices. Despite its reliance on such otherwise irregular practices, fence-breaking's initial success effectively legit-imized the transition from central planning.

Overall, the 1966–1968 and 1979–1989 experiments were similar in their fence-breaking nature, that is, socioeconomic and political forces *within* the state socialist system itself acted in response to the system's shortcomings. However, efforts in the two periods differed in scope, scale, and process. The Vinh Phuc experiment was limited to the agricultural sector, while the 1979–1989 experiment encompassed multiple economic sectors, though without coordination among them. Likewise, the Vinh Phuc experiment was limited to one province, while the 1979–1989 experiment spanned a large number of provinces in both northern and southern Vietnam. Finally, the Vinh Phuc experiment ended without creating any spill-over effects, while the 1979–1989 experiment mustered socioeconomic and political coalitions in favor of *đổi mới* and had an enduring impact on the VCP's decision-making process.

2.2.2 Drivers for Change

Contrary to top-down and bottom-up approaches emphasizing the role either of leadership or of grassroots-level actors in propelling change, the transition in Vietnam exhibits endorsement of change by coalitions of socioeconomic and political forces across sectors and provinces. This collective action of both "masses and elites" took place within a decentralized socialist regime that had resulted from the loosening of political control and the rise of a hybrid structure combining both planned and market-based features.

Supporters consisted of at least four socioeconomic groups with similar perspectives on the potential benefits of change. The first group was production units such as state-operated enterprises and cooperatives already engaged in or benefitting from fence-breaking. The second group was state officials in charge of managing production units. Given that SOEs were under the management of central ministries, provinces, and districts, as owning agencies these institu-tions saw the potential benefit of *đổi mới*. The third comprised those Party-affiliated think tanks that contributed to debates on socialist development or advised the leadership, and the fourth was the top political leadership. There have been no detailed studies on these *đổi mới* coalitions, but the development of these groups can be discerned from various studies on economic and political development between 1975 and 1989 (Thayer, 1988; Riedel & Turley, 1999; Vasavakul, 1999a; Đặng Phong, 2009a).

Citizens *cum* producers were key drivers. Under state socialism the bargain-ing power of rural producers and enterprise workers largely attached to their membership in production units. For example, collective bargaining power in rural areas was possible as cooperatives provided members with some degree of self-government, equality, and food security (Vasavakul, 1999a). This socio-economic group did not have clear connections with the VCP.

Line ministries and provinces, as owning agencies, were attracted to commer-cialized interests derived from fence-breaking. Thus they rendered support to SOEs under their jurisdiction. This is particularly the case with the Ministry of Light Industry, the Ministry of Foreign Trade, and provincial authorities with connections to SOEs engaged in manufacturing. Politically, line ministries and provinces were affiliated with the VCP power structure and were thus in a position to share fence-breaking experiences with decision makers (Vasavakul, 1997). In his study of the Sixth National Party Congress, Carl Thayer confirms the growth of secondary party cadres in the VCP's Central Committee second echelon party cadre, with an increase to 49% from 30% in the previous congress (Thayer, 1988: 187). David Elliott confirms that provincial party leaders totalled 41 out of 173 delegates (23.7%) on the Sixth Congress Central Committee, an increase of 15.6% from the Fifth Congress (Elliott, 1992: 162).

Technocrats who staffed party departments, worked for the Prime Minister, or staffed state-funded research agencies were also drivers of *đổi mới* in their role as think-tank participants. In 1985, the VCP set up an official think tank appointing members from different party and state agencies to review pressing issues (Đặng Phong, 2009b).[4] They collected and formulated data on socialist development experiences at home and abroad and contributed to drafting official policy documents such as resolutions, decrees, and directives. These technocrats worked collectively, though somewhat anonymously.

Similarly, a handful of VCP leaders at the provincial and central levels also actively supported the change agenda. Võ Văn Kiệt, Party Chief of Ho Chi Minh City, facilitated initiatives related to SOEs as well as the aforementioned experiments with price reform in the City. Central-level party leaders also played a critical role in endorsing such experiments as the use of market-driven pricing in the state trading system in Long An, and for the price of rice in An Giang in 1978. They even initiated changes themselves, such as the partial price reform in 1981 (Beresford & Tran, 2004:7). Leadership support

---

[4] At the central level, the key units were the Committee for the Study of New Mechanisms (*Ban cơ chế mới*) set up by the Politburo, the Research Group on Commodity Products and the Law of Value (*nhóm nghiên cứu sản xuất hàng hóa và quy luật giá trị*) set up by the Council of Ministers, the Research Group for the Ministry of Foreign Affairs (*nhóm nghiên cứu của Bộ Ngoại giao*) set up by the Minister of Foreign Affairs, and the Sub-Committee for the Research of Urgent Solutions on Finance, Money, and Prices (*Tiểu ban nghiên cứu giải pháp cấp bách về Tài chính-Tiền tệ-Giá cả*). Contributions from these think tanks served as a foundation for the *đổi mới* agenda (Đặng Phong, 2009b).

continued in 1986, when, with the passing of General Secretary Lê Duẩn in July, Trường Chinh, then Chairman of the State Council, took over until the Sixth National Party Congress in December. Simultaneously assuming both the position of General Secretary and of Chairman of the State Council, Trường Chinh supported the *đổi mới* agenda and its official integration into the Political Report (Đặng Phong, 2009b).

While *đổi mới* can be attributed to coalitions of supporters, not all socio-economic and political groups survived the Sixth Party Congress as coherent social forces. What peasants gained from de-collectivization economically, for example, they lost politically. Under socialism, resistance to socialist economic policies had occurred within the cooperative sector, where the uniformity of the system made individually orchestrated acts of noncompliance powerful throughout that system. Comparing Vietnamese and Chinese labor regimes, Chan and Norlund (1999) point out that the transition from central planning in Vietnam was coupled with recognition of the autonomy of the Vietnam General Confederation of Labor and the increasing role of labor unions in representing workers in disputes. However, under a market system with management power decentralized to enterprises and with unions absent from foreign enterprise, labor union and worker bargaining power *vis-à-vis* management declined (Greenfield, 1994; Vasavakul, 1999a).

Adam Fforde observes that, for their part, the SOEs performed rather well in the 1990s. They were able to generate earnings that allowed them to survive, although their activities were unplanned given that the traditional planning methods had ceased to exist. Fforde concludes that by 1992, SOEs became commercialized entities participating in a range of joint ventures and seeking to meet a variety of goals assigned to them by their owning agencies (Fforde, 2004: 6, 25). Vietnamese technocrats and intellectuals also fared reasonably well. These groups benefitted from the political opening that followed the Sixth Congress. It was not uncommon for those with connections to the party and state power structure to continue in their think tank roles through formal and informal channels.

Key provincial-level officials involved in the *đổi mới* process were appointed to leadership positions. Well-known participants included Võ Văn Kiệt, Ho Chi Minh City Party Secretary, who later assumed the position of Prime Minister; Đoàn Duy Thành, Party Secretary of Hai Phong City, who later served as Deputy Prime Minister; Nguyễn Văn Chính, Party Secretary of Long An, who later served as Deputy Prime Minister; and Nguyễn Văn Hơn, Party Secretary of An Giang, who went on to serve as Deputy Minister of the Ministry of Agriculture (Đặng Phong, 2009a: 15–6). Unlike its socialist counterparts in the Soviet Bloc, the VCP survived its economic transition process and continues to remain a dominant political force. Nonetheless, the *đổi mới* process had the spill-over effect of changing central–local power relations within the VCP and the state administrative apparatus.

2.3 Negotiating a Multi-Sector Economy

Although the Sixth National Party Congress endorsed the coexistence of state and non-state economic sectors, institutionalizing the multi-sector economy has been an ongoing process spanning six national party congresses and government terms so far. Key VCP leaders continue to favor the dominant position of the state sector. Ideological disagreements among VCP leaders have delayed the development of legal frameworks along with the commitments necessary to institution building.

Between the Sixth and the Seventh National Party Congresses (1986–1991), the VCP leaders contended over post–central-planning economic orientation. Their disagreement was reflected in the ideological dissonance between two documents prepared in 1991 prior to the Seventh National Party Congress: the VCP's *Program on the Building of the Country during the Transition to Socialism* (*Cương lĩnh xây dựng đất nước trong thời kỳ quá độ lên chủ nghĩa xã hội*) and the government's *Strategy for Socio-Economic Stabilization and Development to the Year 2000* (*Chiến lược ổn định và phát triển kinh tế xã hội đến năm 2000).*[5] The *Program* asserted that Vietnam was in the process of a transition to socialism and would adopt the strategy that promoted a commodity-based multi-sector economy with socialist orientation (*kinh tế hàng hóa nhiều thành phần theo định hướng xã hội chủ nghĩa*) as a stepping-stone to a more advanced economy driven by industry, services, and agriculture. Socialist orientation was to be concretized in the form of public ownership of the key means of production and the liberation of production forces from exploitation and injustice. The state sector would lead the economy while the private capitalist sector would engage in economic activities for better livelihoods.

The *Strategy*, in stark contrast, downplayed Marxist rhetoric of class struggle and exploitation and defined socialism as a system that would enrich people, create a strong modern country, and build a society where the people were in control. The *Strategy* envisioned a fully developed, well-coordinated market economy, autonomy for SOEs based on the rule of law, and a state committed to

---

[5] The VCP's *Program* was further elaborated in 2011. That same year, the government promulgated a second strategy, the *Strategy for Promoting Socialist-Oriented Industrialization and Modernization to Serve as a Foundation for Vietnam to Become an Industrialized Country by 2020.*

creating a favorable environment for economic development. The *Strategy* delegated to the state sector the key role in the areas that other economic sectors lacked capacity to engage. Overall, the two documents thus put forth two very different approaches for post–central-planning and institution-building.

After the Seventh National Party Congress in 1991, the VCP leadership internally debated the role of the state economic sector, private-sector development, and the role of the state in management. General Secretary Đỗ Mười (1991–1997) represented the views of the coalitions committed to strengthening the orientation adopted in the *Program*. At the Mid-Term National Party Conference in January 1994, Đỗ Mười discussed four dangers confronting Vietnam: economic regression, deviation from socialism, corruption and social evils, and, pejoratively, "peaceful evolution" (*diễn biến hòa bình*). Among these dangers, deviation from socialism and peaceful evolution were the most critical as they would in the long-run enable the rise of socioeconomic classes capable of threatening regime stability.

On the other hand, Prime Minister Võ Văn Kiệt (1991–1997) was more committed to a full transition to a market economy and private sector development. In 1995, prior to the Eighth National Party Congress, Kiệt sent a letter to the Politburo expressing his views on the nature of the international system, the meaning of socialist orientations and deviations, reform of the state system, and reform of the party. Kiệt contended that international relations were no longer characterized by a confrontation between socialism and imperialism. Downplaying the importance of socialist comradeship, he rejected the prospect that communist and international working class movements in the former Soviet Union and Eastern Europe would resurface. Following the spirit of the *Strategy*, Kiệt described socialist orientations as featuring a prosperous people, a strong nation, and an equitable and civilized society. Kiệt contended that the development of the state economic sector was not indicative of a socialist orientation. He emphasized reform in the state system, proposing a complete separation of economic production activities from state management tasks. Kiệt also criticized the Party leadership style and argued for the need to grant autonomy to executive and juridical agencies, elected bodies, and mass organizations. Kiệt asserted in conclusion that democratic centralism had to be replaced by democracy within the Party. Later, Kiệt's letter was leaked to the public (Vasavakul, 1997).

Kiệt's concern over private-sector development and the need for the state actively to create favorable conditions for it was valid. Since the official launch of *đổi mới* in 1986, only limited legal frameworks supported private sector development. Available statistics confirm that as of 1995, SOEs continued to dominate the economy. In January of that year, there were 6,019 SOEs (23.2%),

13,532 private enterprises (52.2%), 5,034 limited liability companies (19.4%), 131 joint-stock companies (0.5%), 926 foreign companies (3.5%), and 270 associated companies (1%). Despite a large number of private enterprises, they constituted only 3.3% of the nation's total capital, as opposed to 85.5% from SOEs (Fforde & Goldstone, 1995:25).

A compromise over how to balance the development of the state and the private economic sector took place in 1997 when the Fourth Plenum of the Central Committee (Eighth Congress) concluded that there was a need to improve efficiency of *all* forms of enterprise. This deliberation became the basis on which the Phan Văn Khải government (1997–2006) prepared the Law on Enterprises of 1999 (applied to both state and private enterprises), drafted a new Land Law, and removed practices listed as economic crimes from the Criminal Code.

Even when Đỗ Mười resigned as General Secretary in 1997, he retained influence over the drafting of legal frameworks for the state sector. In 2000, in his capacity as advisor, he criticized the Phan Văn Khải government for narrowing down the scale of the state economic sector. In 2001, the Resolution of the Third Plenum of the Ninth Party Central Committee (Ninth Congress) introduced the notion of "economic groups" (*tập đoàn kinh tế*) that could compete internationally and thus support Vietnam's global integration. Earlier during his term, Prime Minister Võ Văn Kiệt had started to pilot the reorganization of SOEs into state general corporations (SGCs) (*tổng công ty nhà nước*) of varying scale and significance. The purpose was to relieve the state administrative agencies of actually having to run the businesses as well as to concentrate state capital. State economic groups (SEGs) were to be organized along the line of conglomerates that combined two or more SGCs and included other various subsidiaries under one parent unit placed under direct management of the Prime Minister. The proposal to consolidate and expand SEGs came from Nguyễn Tấn Dũng, then Vice-Prime Minister in charge of the economy and the Head of the Steering Committee for State-Owned Enterprise Innovation and Development from 1997–2006. The Tenth National Party Congress that met in April 2006 endorsed the expansion of SEGs. During the two terms of Prime Minister Nguyễn Tấn Dũng (2006–2016), SEGs and SGCs received priority investment and were considered drivers of Vietnam's economic growth (Vu Thanh Tu Anh, 2017).

The persistence of the state sector in the context of a multi-sector economy arose from a combination of factors. Ideologically, because socialism was associated with public ownership of the means of production, Vietnam's socialist-oriented market economy necessarily included the state sector. At a practical level, the state sector had functioned as the channel for development, resource allocation, and accumulation. De-collectivization of agriculture in 1988, observe Adam Fforde and Anthony Goldstone, made cooperative cadres redundant and politically weakened the party network at the local level. It is thus likely that the party did not want to face a similar loss of control in other sectors (Fforde & Goldstone, 2005: 26, 99–110). Studying Vietnam's access to the WTO, Vu Thanh Tu Anh (2017) argues that party and state leadership had considered WTO accession a threat and thus supported the strengthening of SEGs and SGCs. Despite state sector underperformance during the term of Prime Minister Nguyễn Tấn Dũng (2006–2016), in 2016 the Twelfth National Party Congress of the VCP reaffirmed the state's leading economic role while nonetheless acknowledging the private economy as a crucial driver of the overall economy (Đảng Cộng sản Việt Nam, 2016).

3 State-Building

Along with its market-oriented principles, Prime Minister Võ Văn Kiệt's 1995 letter to the Politburo devoted a section to the role of the state. Kiệt commented on poor performance in state management with particular attention to Vietnam's weak legal frameworks and a lack of legal compliance among state agencies in the performance of their functions. Kiệt also criticized redundancies and bottlenecks in state management on the one hand and widespread problems of "illegal" economic activities on the other. In his analysis, the challenge to the state apparatus arose primarily from state officials' excessive devotion to enterprise at the expense of their state management functions.

To improve efficiency, Kiệt mapped a three-pronged strategy: restructure the state apparatus, reform macroeconomic management, and develop market institutions. Kiệt emphasized the need to first abandon the system of agency-owned state enterprises, or *chủ quản*, and to re-focus the state apparatus exclusively on its management functions. This process would be carried out as an element of public administration reform. Improvements in state management capacity needed to combine with systematic application of the law, and the emerging law-based state, in turn, would be in a position to strengthen its role in macroeconomic management and develop market institutions (Vasavakul, 1997).

Kiệt's comments summarized Vietnam's post–central-planning challenges well. The transition from plan to market that unfolded between 1979 and 1989 gave rise to a decentralized state despite preserving the formal trappings of one-party rule. The state-building project that followed reflected the central state's attempt to rebuild its apparatus and re-centralize political and economic power. The center invoked the concept of the rule of law and uniform public administration while conceding *de facto* decentralization. Vietnam's process of state-building in the post–central-planning era was a protracted one, influenced by contention within the VCP over the role of the post–central-planning state as well as by the dynamics of the multi-sector economy in which the state economic sector played a leading role.

3.1 Transition and the Disintegration of the Socialist State Apparatus and Power

Five dimensions illustrate the impact of transition on the state apparatus: a weakening of vertical ties, the rise of provinces as drivers for growth within the state apparatus, lawlessness among citizens and state officials, the emergence of social connection as a means of rule, and the persistence of commercialized interests within the state apparatus. These dimensions were not mutually exclusive. They reinforced one another to undermine the central state's economic and political power, while contributing to the consolidation of power within local-level state agencies

First, so-called fence-breaking practices in the 1980s weakened hierarchical relationships established during the central planning period. Such practices undercut vertical channels of resource allocation between the State Planning Commission, central ministries, sub-national line agencies, and production units. For example, under central planning a local bank was not responsible for providing foreign currency to local SOEs. Rather, it was the State Planning Commission's responsibility to channel resources through a line ministry for transfer to a provincial line agency, which would in turn confer them on the appropriate enterprise. Similarly, the Provincial Director of the Department of Foreign Trade had no mandate to import production inputs for SOEs, this responsibility being held instead by the central Ministry. Fence-breaking reconfigured these channels and fostered nontraditional, horizontal relations among state agencies and enterprises (Vasavakul, 1996).

Second, the transition process had the effect of strengthening the economic and political position of Vietnam's provinces within the state structure, bypassing the district level advocated by General Secretary Lê Duẩn's large-scale socialist development strategy (Werner, 1988). This rise of province power can be seen in the increase in the number of provinces, their incremental expansion of authority, and the enhanced political position of provincial Party Secretaries within the VCP leadership structure. The reunified Vietnam of 1975 had 72 provinces. By 1978, the VCP had endorsed the merger of 72 provinces into 39 in accordance with the goal of large-scale socialist development. After the Sixth National Party Congress, however, and in conjunction with the overall trend of decentralization, provinces were successively split into smaller units: 44 in 1989, 53 in 1991, 61 in 1997, and 63 in 2008 (*Vietnamnet*, 7 September 2017). Provincial representation in the VCP Central Committee has accordingly increased, from 15.6% of Central Committee members at the Fifth National Congress (1982), to 23.7% at the Sixth Party Congress (1986), 35% at the Seventh Congress (1991), down slightly to 31.2% at the Eighth National Congress (1996), and at the Ninth Congress (2001), 56 of 61 Party Secretaries were members of the Central Committees – over 37% of the total VCP Central Committee membership. From the Seventh Congress in 1991 party chiefs from Ho Chi Minh City and Hanoi were elected members of the Politburo (Thayer, 1988; Riedel & Turley, 1999; Huy Đức, 2012). The rise of provincial power in the 1990s went hand in hand with delegation of responsibility to the local state structure. The first key management sectors decentralized to local state agencies were land, foreign direct investment, and budget as seen in the frameworks of the Land Law (1993 and 2003), the Law on Foreign Investment (1996), and the State Budget Law (1996 and 2002). These initial devolved responsibilities have indeed enabled some local state agencies to act as development drivers.

Third, the transition process took place without the concurrent development of any institutional or legal frameworks. This lack posed a major challenge to the central state in directing post–central-planning development and holding local states accountable. More often than not, local state agencies were left at liberty to exercise discretionary power in state management. In the 1990s, the dispersal of the central state's powers was typified in the Vietnamese press through slogans such as "the emperor's edict stops at the provincial gate" (*phép vua thua lệ tỉnh*) and "the upper echelon commands but the lower echelon does not listen" (*trên bảo dưới không nghe*). Indeed, in 1995 alone the Supreme People's Organ of Control had to file objections against over 300 documents issued by provincial-level authorities and over 600 from wards and districts in conflict with central regulations, and the Minister of Agriculture and Rural Development reported to the National Assembly that over half of Vietnam's provinces did not complete and return land-use plans as requested (Vasavakul, 1996 and 1999). Central–local state relations were further complicated by Vietnam's one-party system, since under the VCP leadership structure ministers and provincial party chiefs both served on the VCP Central Committee and were thus politically equal, making it an alien notion that provincial states would be administratively subordinate to central ministries.

Fourth, the transition process in rural Vietnam, culminating in de-collectivization in the 1980s, had a major impact on the state apparatus in the countryside where some 80% of the population resided. It was during this time that the rural cooperative, which had assumed socioeconomic and management functions, disintegrated. In its place individual farmers, households, and the farmers' groups known as "cooperation groups" (*tổ hợp tác*) became drivers for local-level economic development independent of any state structure (Vasavakul & Nguyen Thai Van, 2006). Politically, meanwhile, the cooperative system's demise left behind a weakened commune-level administration to assume full state-management functions. Many communes revived the traditional structure of the "village" (*thôn*) organized along residential clusters to facilitate the reach of the state. At the grassroots level the household (*hộ gia đình*) re-emerged as a socioeconomic and cultural institution, placing renewed importance on familial and lineage relations (*dòng họ*) as social institutions. In the Red River Delta, for example, ancestral shrines, lineage records, and lineage-based charity organizations became signs of heritable socioeconomic status and power. In lieu of formal rules and regulations, local authorities and households resorted to the traditional social contract mechanism known as "*hương ước*" (often translated as "village convention") to govern state–community and intracommunity relations. The nebulous nature of central state power at the grassroots level persisted throughout the 1990s (Vasavakul, 1999).

Finally, the transition process catalyzed the growth of commercial interests within the state apparatus across sociopolitical levels and economic sectors. Increasingly, state officials came to regard state positions, policies, and power as means for promoting commercial interests, and so naturally the concerns of such interests increasingly took precedence over state management priorities (Vasavakul, 1996 and 1999).

Under the state socialist economic system, the central state agencies, following central planning principles, had controlled state assets and their use, formulated plans for cumulative growth, and allocated resources for plan targets. In addition, following the principles of socialism, the state had not only engaged in economic management but also assumed social welfare functions. As a result of fence-breaking during the transition period, the central state's economic powers diminished, devolving to sub-national levels. The simultaneous commercialization of the state apparatus had the effect of shifting state agencies' focus to generating wealth at the expense of other social welfare functions, and opportunities to acquire wealth at the local level multiplied in the absence of formal legal frameworks, opening up opportunities for the use of horizontal social connections as alternatives. The weakening of vertical relations and the absence of formal rules loosened central state political control while contributing to the consolidation of power within local-level state agencies. In a nutshell, the socialist regime had, to a large extent, disintegrated.

In this context of state disintegration and given that VCP members had continued to assume key positions in the state structure, the VCP took initiatives to recentralize intraparty control. The Third Plenum of the Central Committee that met in 1997 introduced a mechanism known as "the rotation of cadres" (*luân chuyển cán bộ*), holding central and local leadership and management positions as an element of personnel planning and promotion. Subsequently, between 1997 and 2002, the Politburo and the Secretariat piloted personnel rotation between the central and the provincial levels, among different provinces, and between the provincial and the district levels. In 2002, Politburo Resolution No. 11-NQ/TW further institutionalized cadre rotation. At the central level, deputy-level ministers and party chiefs were rotation targets; provincial-level targets included the Party and People's Committee executive tier and Standing Committee members. The resolution also mandated rotating secondary central department heads and such out to provincial departments and district offices. Rotation became a promotion requirement during party congresses, which, in turn, affected appointments to state positions. Party documents stated that cadre rotation not only served to elevate the professional expertise of potential leaders but also cemented central–provincial ties. In practice, cadre rotation has enabled VCP leaders to promote supporters in their networks to high-ranking party and state positions.

3.2 The Making of the State Apparatus

The VCP and various governments also addressed challenges to the generally problematic authority of the state through national-level programs aimed at reforming both the state's structure and its management role. This process came to be known as public administration reform (PAR). The term "public administration" (*hành chính công*) was new for Vietnam and reflected conceptual influences outside the socialist circle of thought (Vasavakul, 2002).

One of the very first concerns of the Võ Văn Kiệt government was to reduce cumbersome administrative procedures inherited from the central planning period. In 1994, the government passed Resolution 38 calling for ministries and provinces to simplify administrative procedures required of citizens and organizations under their managerial jurisdiction. This move reflected a practical concern with issues of bureaucratic red tape inherited from the central planning period, along with the perceived urgency of reforming state management functions by reducing the state's regulatory role. In 1995, the Eighth Plenum of the Central Committee (Eighth Congress) endorsed a notion of public administration reform comprising three components: administrative-procedural, organizational, and civil-service. In 2001, Prime Minister Phan Văn Khải approved the Master Program on Public Administration Reform (PAR-MP) for the 2001–2010 period, addressing institutional, organizational, public financial, and civil service reform. In 2011, the Nguyễn Tấn Dũng government endorsed a subsequent master program to cover the 2011 to 2020 period. The original focus on reducing red tape had been integrated into the institutional reform component (Vasavakul, 2002 and 2012).

Fundamentally, these reform programs advocated building uniformity within the state structure by imposing a unified organizational structure while concurrently institutionalizing apportionment of management respon-sibilities between central and local state agencies. The reform programs also addressed certain specific functions of the state related to planning and legal drafting.

3.2.1 Reorganizing the State Apparatus

The first key measure adopted in the process of state restructuring was a reduction in size of the state apparatus inherited from the central planning period. At that time, Vietnam reportedly had some seventy ministries, state commissions, general departments, and agencies directly subordinated to the Council of Ministries, and a total of 850 departments and institutes. Each province had thirty-four to forty offices of central state organs with hundreds of subordinate sections. Many of these offices extended down to the district level (Porter, 1993: 78–9). Throughout the 1990s and 2000s, seventy or so ministries thinned to twenty-two ministries and seven ministry-level agencies during the Võ Văn Kiệt government, and these numbers shrank further to eighteen ministries and four ministry-level agencies during the second term of Nguyễn Tấn Dũng, a structure so far retained by the Nguyễn Xuân Phúc government (2016–present) (SRV Government web portal).

In the *đời mới* era, ministries are for the most part new creations. Government researchers and practitioners have adopted the so-called multi-sectoral, multi-functional (*đa ngành đa lĩnh vực*) approach to ministerial reorganization (Văn Tất Thu, 2007). In the 1990s, ministries inherited from the central planning period underwent major restructuring. The current Ministry of Planning and Investment, for example, results from reorganizing the State Planning Commission and the investment and assistance cooperation sector, once under the jurisdiction of the former Ministry of Foreign

Economics. Later, the General Bureau of Statistics was folded into the Ministry as well. As a result of these mergers, each ministry can now oversee more than one sector, widening its range of economic, social, and managerial functions (Vasavakul et al., 2009).

The structure of the sub-national state more or less follows the restructuring at the central level. All provinces were required to set up a fixed set of general management and line departments, although the number of public service delivery units and SOEs could vary from province to province. Line agencies at the provincial level have operated on the principle of "dual subordination" (*song trùng trực thuộc*). They are subordinated to central ministries in areas of technical work (*ngành dọc*) while simultaneously subordinated to the Provincial People's Committee in regard to territorial management (*ngành ngang*). The exceptions are sectors such as taxation, customs, state treasury, and security, where sub-national line agencies are directly subordinated to central ministries (Vasavakul, 2012).

State reorganization also meant strengthening commune-level administration. Seen as essential to linking local government with citizens, this move was endorsed by the Fifth Plenum of the Central Committee in 2002. Since 2004, the Ministry of Home Affairs (MOHA)'s guidelines have institutionalized the structure of commune-level administration as well as its system of public officials. The guidelines also clarify the status of units under the commune. The rural hamlet and the urban residential unit are not administrative levels but are self-managed local community units even while falling under the commune's administrative responsibility. Overall, in the era of *đổi mới*, the commune-level administration has been restored and strengthened to serve as the basic-level administration in the absence of the socialist cooperative system (Vasavakul, 2012).

The structural reorganization process took place in conjunction with the redefinition of the role of the state, the key focus being the separation of economic and public service delivery from state management functions. To reduce the state role in the direct management of SOEs, the VCP and the government clarified the notion of ownership representation and its separation from SOE management functions. To separate public services from state management, in the 1990s, the VCP and the government introduced "socialization" (*xã hội hóa*), broadly defined as participation of the private sector and communities in providing public services beyond fee payment. In the era of *đổi mới*, legal frameworks for financial mechanisms and management models have concretized socialization for public service delivery units (London, 2011).

3.2.2 Management Decentralization

After state downsizing under *đổi mới*, the second key measure in Vietnam's state restructuring process focused on clarifying central and local state agencies' responsibilities. In 2004, Resolution 8 institutionalized state management decentralization. The stipulations of Resolution 8 were not entirely new; rather, they affirmed decentralization trends that had already developed, further institutionalizing already *de facto* decentralization practices. Nonetheless, it should be noted that earlier decentralization practices had failed to guarantee a unified management (*chưa đảm bảo quản lý thống nhất*), had become dispersed (*phân tán*), had created factional clusters (*cục bộ*), and had weakened administrative discipline (*kỷ cương hành chính chưa nghiêm*). These problems evinced a lack of clear delineation of responsibilities and jurisdiction at each administrative level (Vasavakul, 1999).

Resolution 8 confirmed the delegation of six clusters of managerial responsibilities to local state agencies: socioeconomic planning and investment; budgeting; land, natural resources, and state property; SOEs; public service units (education, health care, sports, and culture); and personnel. While the central government delegated responsibilities to the provinces, the provincial-level People's Committee and People's Council decided on the scheme for decentralization to lower administrative echelons.[6]

Under Resolution 8 decentralization of planning focused broadly on four types: socioeconomic, foreign direct investment (FDI), public investment, and spatial. Decentralization of socioeconomic planning took place in conjunction with the establishment of the Ministry of Planning and Investment (MPI) in 1996. While the MPI has continued to assign plan activities and targets to ministries and provinces, central and local agencies rely on decentralized functions to elaborate their own detailed plans (Lê Viết Thái, 2012). Decentralization of FDI planning took place from 1997–2006. While until 2006, provinces evaluated and licensed FDI projects according to the capital amount and the area of investment, since then the MPI has removed limits on investment size even while continuing to submit projects of national importance for the Prime Minister's approval (Nguyễn Mại, 2012; Vu Thanh Tu Anh, 2016). Prior to 2003, central state agencies governed all public investment projects, but between 2003 and 2006 decision making decentralized, based on public investment project scale and type. Since then, the majority of public

---

[6] In addition to Resolution 8, other decentralization frameworks applied to selected units of municipalities under the central government, certain economic zones, and the capital city. This Element does not discuss these trends.

investment projects have been decentralized to sectors and provinces. The Prime Minister has only retained authority over strategically important and large-scale projects (Trần Du Lịch, 2014). Finally, since 2008, decentralization in the domain of spatial planning has focused on the development of nation-wide infrastructure such as transportation, economic and industrial zones, irrigation and water, waste management, hospitals, and education facilities. Ministries and people's committees formulate spatial plans. The MPI's ability to control and coordinate this domain has been limited, as Vietnam does not have national frameworks for it. Additionally, while ministries and provinces report to the MPI and its line agency on preparation, appraisal, and approval of spatial plans, they are not required to report on implementation (Lê Viết Thái, 2012). Overall, the decentralization of planning is extensive, while the ability of central government agencies to control locally engendered plans and implementation has been limited given the absence of national-level plans.

In addition to the planning decentralization of the 1990s, budgetary decentralization unfolded in Vietnam from 1989 to 2015, increasing local governments' share in total national revenue collections and expenditures. The Council of Ministers' Resolution No. 186-HDBT of 1989 outlines revenue collection sources and expenditures of the local government while the 1996 Budget Law specifies the division of rights and responsibilities related to revenue and expenditure between central and provincial governments as well as among different levels of local government. The 2002 legal framework elaborates seven key budgetary functions: state budget estimation, spending norms and regulations, revenue and spending tasks, consolidation and formulation of state budget plans, execution of state budget plans, accounting, and formulation and approval of the finalization of state budget reports. Additionally, provinces receive transfers from the central government and may also borrow domestically provided that they meet certain requirements. The 2002 budget law increased the proportion of local collections. Excluding revenue collected from enterprises in the oil and gas sector, local collections averaged 44% of revenue collection in Vietnam between 2004 and 2008. The proportion of central transfers dropped to an average of 34.1% between 2005 and 2010. Local spending rose from an average of 37.9% in 1996–2000 to 47.2% in 2008 and over 50% of total spending in 2009–2010 (Vũ Sỹ Cường, 2012).

Yet overall, budgetary decentralization has focused mainly on the delegation of collection and spending implementation designed by central agencies, not the devolution of collection and spending decisions. The system thus does not conduce to revenue development at the local level. Given the absence of linkages between planning and budgeting, the system encourages "asking and giving" practices familiar from the central planning era. The most recent budget law, passed in 2015 (effective from the 2017 fiscal year), attempts to correct existing shortcomings by allocating a larger share of collections to provinces. At the same time, it strengthens fiscal discipline at the provincial level, specifying the maximum level of debt that provincial governments can mobilize. (Nguyen Thi Thuy, 2016).

The Land Law frameworks from 1993 to 2003 divided land-management responsibilities among central, provincial, and district state agencies. The 1993 framework allowed district state agencies to manage agricultural land used by households and individuals while assigning provincial state agencies the task of determining the use of agricultural land by organizations and in plots under one hectare. It left the use of nonagricultural land beyond the authority of the province to the central government's discretion. The revised 1998 law further reduced the scope of central state authority over land designation for defense and infrastructure purposes. The amended Land Law of 2001 assigned districts the responsibility to issue land use permits for households and individuals and reserved the issuance of urban land use permits to their provinces. The 2003 Land Law devolved land use planning to various sub-national administrative levels pending approval from the upper echelon. Additionally, while the Ministry of Finance determined a framework for land pricing, provinces decided on a list of land prices when they had to calculate compensation for land acquired for national purposes, land use rights fees, rents of public land, and the price of land when corporatizing SOEs (Ngân hàng Thế giới, 2012; Đặng Hùng Võ, 2012; Châu Hoàng Thân, 2018).

Regarding the management of SOEs, decentralization followed the guidelines provided in the resolutions of the Third Plenum of the Central Committee in 2001, the Laws on State Enterprises of 2003 and 2005, and related implementation decrees. Basically, the government decentralizes the management of state ownership rights over SOEs to line ministries, People's Committees, the Ministry of Finance, or SOE Management Councils, which make decisions on reorganization, strategy, and investment planning. The central government reviews and approves reorganization proposals but could further delegate decision-making authority based on the level of investment capital (Trần Tiến Cường, 2012).

In the area of public service delivery, the provincial state, following the stipulations of the 2002 Budget Law, has been assigned spending responsibility for human-development services, especially education and health care. Central ministries have delegated provincial, district, and commune-level state agencies to manage schools and health facilities. Local state agencies are also responsible for promoting socialization (*xã hội hóa*) – that is, organizing contributions and participation from community members *cum* end-users beyond fee payment to include society's direct involvement in service-delivery development.

Finally, Resolution 8 has confirmed the delegation of select organizational and personnel management functions to local state agencies. MOHA has continued to enforce a unified organizational structure for the state apparatus, although it has allowed provinces to make minor adjustments depending on local conditions. Regarding personnel management, VCP central agencies have continued to control appointments to leadership positions. Specifically, the Politburo decides on provincial Party Secretaries, Chairs of the People's Councils, and the People's Committees of Hanoi and Ho Chi Minh City. The VCP Secretariat decides on chairs of the provincial People's Councils and People's Committees, while the Central Committee is consulted on the appointment of certain leadership positions. MOHA has continued to determine numbers of civil servants in central and local state agencies but has granted provinces the authority to determine staffing for service delivery professionals in education and healthcare. While MOHA has set up a framework to recruit civil servants and service-delivery professionals, it has delegated those tasks to ministries and provincial-level People's Committees (Vasavakul, 2012).

Overall, Resolution 8 has institutionalized decentralization trends since the 1990s. Vietnam's decentralization scheme has adopted an "equality" approach, making no major distinction between rich and poor, urban and rural, or Kinh-majority and minority provinces. It was not until the passage of the 2013 Constitution and the subsequent passage in 2015 of the Laws on Government Organization and Local Government that there has been a move toward differentiating rural from urban governance.

3.3 Law, Plan, Program, and Policy in State Management

The restructuring of the state apparatus went hand in hand with VCP and government attempts to clarify state adherence to rule of law, plan, and policy. In the era of *đổi mới*, the VCP and the government adopted the principle of a law-based state (*nhà nước pháp trị/nhà nước pháp quyền*). Concurrently, central and local states have continued to use plans as management tools. The notion of "policy" has only recently been introduced into the *đổi mới* discourse, mostly through exchanges among technocrats, researchers, and NGOs. In varying degrees, law, plan, and policy are reference points for state management in the era of *đổi mới*.

Throughout the 1990s, various state agencies produced distinct types of legal documents. More often than not, these documents were not implementable because of conflicting contents and lack of guiding detail. Furthermore, citizens were mostly unaware of the documents' guiding rationale or even existence. The Ministry of Justice has since attempted to unify and standardize the drafting of legal documents. These efforts are reflected in a series of Laws on the Promulgation of the Legal Documents passed by the National Assembly in 1996, 2004, 2008, and 2015. The process of unification and standardization has been incremental.

The 2008 Law on the Promulgation of Legal Documents was a leap forward in setting out essential, standardized directions. First, it confirmed the decentralization of legal promulgation while reducing the variety of legal documents. It permitted each agency to issue only one type: the Government and Head of the State Audit of Vietnam could issue decrees (*nghị định*); the Prime Minister could issue decisions (*quyết định*); and Ministries and Heads of the Procuracy or Supreme Court could issue circulars (*thông tư*). At the local level, in the context of management decentralization, provincial People's Committees could issue implementation guidelines. Second, the law required the drafting committee to produce a Regulatory Impact Assessment detailing and appraising the potential impact of any new regulation. Third, it required that the parent document and detailed legal documents be promulgated together to ensure coordination and consistency. Finally, the 2008 Law mandated public disclosure of all drafts sixty days before the drafts were passed, to facilitate public consultation for final revision. Aligning with the 2013 Constitutional frameworks, the 2015 Law on Promulgation of Legal Documents adjusted the types of legal documents and included elaborate details on the collection of public opinion during the drafting process, with emphasis on transparency in the receipt of and response to public comments and proposals.

Despite the increasing significance of the rule of law, at the operational level the Vietnamese state has continued to rely on spatial plans (*quy hoạch*) and socioeconomic development plans (*kế hoạch*) as management tools. Additionally, state agencies continue to frame their specific actions and solutions in the form of programs (*chương trình*) and projects (*dự án*) on, for example, poverty reduction, rural development and climate change, or infrastructure development. Yet, given that Vietnam has no national-level master plan connecting frameworks for sectoral and provincial plans, plan implementation remains un-coordinated.

Increasingly, Vietnamese researchers, technocrats, and NGOs have begun to use the term "policy" (*chính sách*) when discussing government decisions, actions, and solutions. The term "policy" is new in the context of one-party rule. In the past, the term was loosely used in connection with the VCP's policy line (*chủ trương chính sách*). The notion of "policy" has been introduced to Vietnam mostly through foreign exchanges. Researchers and technocrats are attracted to the easily accessible policy-analysis methods gained through these exchanges, while NGOs consider "policy advocacy" (*vận động chính sách*) a strategy for change. NGOs mostly conduct "policy advocacy" when engaged in law-drafting. However, researchers, technocrats, and NGOs have not established clear connections between laws, plans, and policies. It remains unclear in the Vietnamese context whether policies should generate laws, plans, and programs or *vice versa*.

Under one-party rule, the executive branch takes the lead in formulating legal frameworks to fill the vacuum left from the central planning period. It also formulates plans. As a result of the executive-driven lawmaking and planning process, legal frameworks more often than not reflect parochial, sectoral, or provincial "policy" interests. Legal stipulations have often been enmeshed with the concerns and interests of actors and groups inside the state apparatus, unbeknownst to those outside it.

3.4 Emerging Fragmented Authority Relations

To a large extent, the VCP-endorsed restructuring of the state has addressed the challenges brought about by the transition process. The restructuring of the state from the central to the commune level has re-established some level of centralized control and nationwide uniformity. Each ministry is now composed of four types of unit. The first type includes general management units for administration, personnel, planning, finance, legal affairs, international relations, and inspection. The second type includes specialized technical units either as departments (*vụ*) or bureaus (*cục*). The third type is affiliated SOEs, and the fourth comprises public service delivery vehicles such as research, education, and training agencies, information technology centers, newspapers, and publishing houses. Management decentralization clarified the division of responsibilities between central and local state agencies, while the institutionalization of decentralized frameworks confirmed *de facto* decentralization, effectively curtailing new "fence-breaking" practices. The government's implementation of public administration reform measures also created a certain level of uniformity within the state structure. This was particularly the case in the clarification of authority in promulgating legal and policy documents, in the reform of state agencies' regulatory role, in the standardization of the administrative budget, and in the reform of the civil service system.

The reorganization of the socialist state has not been without structural challenges. The state apparatus in the era of *đổi mới* has remained cumbersome. The merger of ministries along the multi-sector and multi-functional principle at the central level has been a mere "mechanical move" (*cơ học*) that physically combined state units without reorganizing their functions. Multi-sectoral and multi-functional approaches have further justified a large number of leadership and staff positions to respond to ensuing work requirements. A report from a monitoring team set up to review the organization of the state apparatus in 2017 observes that from 2007 to 2017, while the structure of the government comprised eighteen ministries, four ministry-level agencies, and eight agencies, in reality, the number of state units within each ministry rose at an alarming rate. Between 2011 and 2016, ministries established a total of twenty-nine units at the bureau level, which, in turn, gave rise to 180 new sub-units (*VOV*, 7 August 2017). A similar trend has also taken place at the sub-national level. According to the Party Central Committee on Organization, the addition of nineteen new provinces between 1989 and 2008 generated 178 more districts and 1,136 more communes (*Vietnamnet*, September 7, 2017). A 2016 MOHA report points out that there were close to 1.3 million civil servants, party and mass organization cadres at the commune and sub-commune (hamlet) levels, all of whom were supported by a state budget reportedly reaching 32,000 billion VND annually (*Báo Đất Việt*, October 17, 2017). Overall, despite attempts to streamline the state apparatus by winnowing central ministries and state agencies, positions to lead and staff the remaining ones have tended to multiply.

At the provincial level, management decentralization has had the effect of strengthening provincial powers within the state structure on one hand and their reliance on central state patronage on the other. With the exception of some responsibilities, delegated in the early 1990s to districts, in managing the land households, individuals, and communities use, survey results obtained from over thirty departments of Home Affairs in 2012 indicated a moderate degree of decentralization from provinces to districts and communes in practice.[7] Provinces strictly followed the fiscal decentralization scheme under the Budget Law of 2002. Of provinces surveyed, 90.5% endorsed financial self-management rights and 88.1% decentralized budget estimation. However, only 69% of the provinces had decentralized investment to districts and communes. Likewise, only 69% confirmed any decentralization of staff recruiting for service-delivery units, and only 50% had decentralized recruitment of local

---

[7] The form, focusing on the implementation of overall and specific PAR measures at the provincial level, was sent to the Department of Home Affairs (DOHA) in sixty-three provinces in March and April 2012. Half of DOHA offices answered.

government officials (Vasavakul 2012). Overall, although the decentralization framework has encouraged the redistribution of responsibilities within each province, local administrative state power remains varyingly concentrated at the provincial level. While management decentralization has expanded the authority of the provincial state, limited decentralization of decision making has encouraged the practice of "asking-giving" (*xin cho*) when provinces seek support and favour from either central ministries or individual state and party officials. Limited resources from the central state budget have also motivated provinces to seek support for local agendas directly from central party-state agencies. Across sectors, this practice has facilitated the rise of patronage networks within the state apparatus.

The development of the rule of law notwithstanding, law making in Vietnam has increasingly become an area of competing interests, first and foremost among state agencies, as those responsible for law and policy drafting become invested in particular outcomes. Ministries and provinces also use plans and programs to advance their specific interests. As the *đổi mới* state structure has neither authoritative national-level coordinating agencies nor national master plans to mediate among competing interests across sectors and provinces, the state apparatus in action has increasingly become fragmented.

3.5 The Political Economy of the *Đổi Mới* Growth Model

In this section, I consider a set of state management areas and economic sectors to illustrate the political economy of the *đổi mới* growth model. The management areas under consideration are public investment, poverty reduction, and local development. The public investment discussion will illustrate patterns of central–local state agency decision making and resource allocation as well as patronage networks that have emerged within the state apparatus. Poverty reduction, one of Vietnam's sixteen national target programs, will shed light on how a national-level program is formulated, how ministries and provinces implement multi-sectoral national target programs, and emerging challenges for management decentralization. The discussion of local development focuses on the two most decentralized sectors of land management and foreign direct investment, examining how provincial states have capitalized on decentralization and how decentralization has affected local state–citizen relations and the dynamics of provincial-level development. The discussion of two particular economic sectors, the state and the private sector (that is, non-state economic actors engaged in nonagricultural activities), recaps the role of both in Vietnam's multi-sector economy. Together, these policy areas help clarify the structural sources of power within the state apparatus, the drivers of *đổi mới*, and the stability of one-party rule.

3.5.1 Public Investment

Public investment programs are understood to cover investment programs carried out by the government and SOEs by means of state budgets (including overseas development assistance), credits guaranteed by the state, government bonds, and investment from SOEs. In the context of decentralization, public investment has been delegated to ministries and provinces, which, in turn, are required to follow steps for proposals, screening, development, appraisal, implementation, and assessment. Ministries and provinces are also to ensure the availability of sources of capital.

Overall, both central and local state agencies have committed to a high level of public investment, particularly in infrastructure. A study from the Fulbright Economics Program based in Ho Chi Minh City observes investment in electricity, water, waste treatment, transport, and communications averaging 9.4% of GDP from 1996 to 2000. Investment increased during the second term of the Phan Văn Khải government to 10.1% from 2001 to 2005. It then climbed even higher to 11.9% of GDP during the 2006–2010 Nguyễn Tấn Dũng government (Vietnam Executive Leadership Program, 2012). This increase is comparable with Taiwan and South Korea, which invested approximately 9% of their GDP in infrastructure over the thirty-year period from 1960 to 1990 (Mody, 1997).

Despite this trend, however, central and local state agencies have apparently favored economic investment and state management investment at the expense of social investment. Records from the MPI show that between 2000 and 2009, economic investment formed 73% of the state budget while human development investment (e.g., science, education, training, health, culture, sports, and social assistance) declined from 17.6% to 5.1%. In particular, public investment for science, education, and training dropped from 8.5% in 2000 to 5.1% in 2009 while health and social assistance, despite a slight increase from 2.4% to 3.9% between 2003 and 2008, plummeted to 2.8% in 2009. Investment for state management was also high, forming some 8% of the budget by 2010 (*Kiểm toán Nhà nước Việt Nam*, August 8, 2012).

The decentralization of public investment and the absence of national and regional-level master plans has had the effect of granting provinces "blank checks" on decision making. According to MPI records, in 2012 Vietnam had 100 seaports, of which 20 were international, and 22 civilian airports, of which 8 were international. As of early 2010 Vietnam was building 18 economic zones for marine products, 30 border economic zones, 260 industrial zones, and 650 smaller industrial clusters (*Kiểm toán Nhà nước Việt Nam*, August 8, 2012). Observers have commented that provincial-level infrastructure investment projects have developed following the "movement" mentality (*theo phong trào*) and as a result may not have been the most cost-efficient. Duplication has taken place, although provinces are able to share seaports and airports as well as higher education institutions (Vũ Khoan, *Kinh tế Saigon Online*, August 12, 2011).

In practice, while ministries and provinces made public investment decisions, limited state resources required that they adopt various strategies to ensure rapid project approval and state funding. Reports from both the Government Inspectorate and the State Audit of Vietnam indicate that it was quite common for heads of responsible state agencies to approve projects under their jurisdiction that did not meet formal requirements. For example, line ministries reportedly approve projects prior to reviewing appraisal reports, while provinces approve projects not aligned with either their strategic master plans or socioeconomic development plans. It was also common that project investors understated cost projections to keep them below the threshold that would trigger mandatory review by higher authorities.

Reports from both the Government Inspectorate and the State Audit of Vietnam indicate a rise in the phenomenon called "*đội vốn,*" that is, continuing to raise capital requirements after project approval. The Government Inspectorate reported a particular spate of such cases between 2010 and 2016, when the City of Hai Phong approved 282 new projects with a total capital of VND 51.2 trillion and made a total of 236 capital adjustments. Likewise, when the Inspectorate carried out detailed reviews of 22 investment projects between 2010 and 2017, it concluded that every project had requested a capital increase. It called special attention to a 2.2-kilometer project to upgrade Road 356, undertaken by the Department of Transportation, that raised its capital requirement from the original VND 314 billion in 2010 to VND 1.311 trillion two years later. The State Audit of Vietnam reported a similar case to the National Assembly, involving the dredging of the Sao Khe River in Ninh Binh Province south of Hanoi. The project's capital budget increased 36 times from an original amount of VND 72 billion to VND 2.6 trillion (*Báo Mới*, June 3, 2018).

Of course, increasing capital budgets after approval was not without its justifications. The Hai Phong People's Committee cited a shortage of capital, inflation, changes in the municipality's master plans, changes in project scope, and mergers of projects to justify its request for an investment capital increase (*VNExpress*, July 17, 2018). Given that most Hai

Phong projects fell under the City's jurisdiction, the People's Committee argued that changes required no reporting. The Party Secretary of Ninh Binh, meanwhile, attributed the rising investment capital requirements in the Sao Khe case to poor design of the original project, the necessary revision of the project scope and mission, and additional costs to cover items such as land clearance and compensation to local inhabitants (*VTC News*, May 23, 2018). With or without justification, however, the phenomenon of capital overruns after approval has been systemic.

Fundamentally, the heads of central and provincial state agencies have authority over the approval and continuation of public investment projects. Vietnam's public investment sector shows that the *đổi mới* state structure is the arena where decision makers and investors negotiate development. Ministries and provinces often seek flexibility when implementing formal legal requirements, justified by varying specific conditions. Central leaders, including the Prime Minister, have adopted the so-called "blank check style" (*kiểu khoán trắng*) for project approval, adjustment, and funding. A study on budgetary allocations interestingly shows that the state budget for public investment has been spread thinly, although quite evenly, across sectors and provinces (Vũ Sỹ Cường et al., 2014).

In the era of *đổi mới*, the asking-and-giving mechanism has been institutionalized. Although informal in nature, it has bypassed other, formal channels. In turn, it has fostered and sustained various forms of vertical, horizontal, and multi-sectoral patronage networks within the state apparatus. Without question, this mechanism and the country's emerging patronage networks have promoted some level of local initiative, leading in turn to economic growth and reinforcing central–local vertical ties; however, its informal pervasiveness has undermined accountability within the state apparatus as well as the effectiveness of state-led public investment.

3.5.2 Poverty Reduction

Poverty reduction is another management area that illustrates how the decentralized state apparatus functions in practice, especially when formulating and implementing multi-sector programs. This management area also indicates emerging governance challenges in the context of decentralization.

The VCP's concern with poverty dates back to 1992, when the Seventh National Party Congress recognized poverty in Vietnam's mountainous provinces as a key problem requiring continuing effort. In the *đổi mới* era, central state agencies have developed national programs to support poor households and communities. The highlights are the Hunger Eradication and Poverty

Reduction Program; Programs for Socio-Economic Development in the Mountainous and Ethnic Minority Regions; the Program on Rapid and Sustainable Poverty Reduction for 64 Poor Districts; the National Target Program for Sustainable Poverty Reduction (2012–2015), and socioeconomic development programs for border areas and for the North Central, Central Coastal, Central Highlands, the Mekong river delta, and Northwestern mountainous regions. These programs have prioritized livelihood improvement, education, health care, legal support, and support for ethnic minority groups.

Multi-sector poverty-reduction programs are coordinated by a national steering committee headed by a Deputy Prime Minister. The Ministry of Labor, War Invalids, and Social Affairs (MOLISA) is the standing agency responsible for managing almost all poverty-reduction programs. Additional participating central ministerial-level state agencies are Planning and Investment; Finance; Agriculture and Rural Development; Education and Training; Health; Transportation; the State Bank of Vietnam; and the Committee on Ethnic Minorities. Mass organizations and civil society organizations have also supported program implementation and monitoring. Provinces also set up steering committees at the provincial, district, and commune levels. Committee members, recruited from relevant line agencies, are responsible for the implementation of the program aspects falling under their jurisdiction. As MOLISA is the lead agency, the DOLISA is assigned as a representative to coordinate poverty implementation at the province level. It is also responsible for synthesizing, managing, and proposing the ways in which a budget should be allocated. While provincial People's Committees are in charge of organizing and managing the program, they have delegated implementation responsibilities to districts as most service delivery providers (extension service centers, education, health care providers) are based at the district level (MOLISA & UNDP, 2004).

So far in the era of *đổi mới*, most of Vietnam's poverty reduction programs have begun with nationwide collection of data on poor households. This work is delegated to the commune-level administration to set up a commune survey committee to gather information that serves as the baseline for program formulation and implementation nationwide and in each locality. Responsible central agencies adopt a semi-participatory approach in formulating program frameworks and specific program focuses. For example, to formulate projects on infrastructure development in mountainous areas, the Committee for Ethnic Minorities Affairs, the key agency responsible, has annually announced available financial capital to all targeted communes. The People's Committees of these communes, with participation from local mass organizations, then determine investment priorities. Each commune subsequently develops a detailed proposal to send to a district steering committee. Proposals the district approves are forwarded to the provincial steering committee for consideration.

Undoubtedly, poverty reduction efforts have brought about impressive results. Vietnam reduced its household poverty rate from 58.1% in 1993 to 13.5% in 2014 per the Vietnam Household Living Standard Survey (using the poverty line defined by the World Bank and Vietnam's General Statistics Office). However, progress has been uneven. A high percentage of the population remains near-poor, and urban poverty has risen. Accounting for just 15% of the population, ethnic minorities account for more than half of the country's poor. Of those in the category "near-poor," 75% live on USD $2–10 per person per day (2005 PPP). Many households in this category are in the informal sector or have small children, elderly, or disabled members. In urban Vietnam, poverty has also emerged among migrants and informal-sector workers (UNDP, 2017).

Poverty-program implementation sheds light on the inner working of the decentralized *đổi mới* state, from the division of responsibilities among state agencies to the role of legal frameworks, resource allocation, and citizen participation. At the provincial level, while DOLISA was originally designated the lead agency, in some provinces its planning and budgeting roles have been taken over by the Department of Planning and Investment and the Department of Finance. Furthermore, planning and implementation have remained centralized at the province and district level despite communes' being responsible for implementation. In connection with the implementation process, poverty reduction programs have generated a large number of legal documents. The credit policy for the rural poor, for example, at one point appeared in 25 separate implementation guidelines, leading to fragmentation of resource allocation and overlapping beneficiaries and areas targeted. Overall, central state resources have been spread thinly across programs, resulting in each program's only partially meeting budget requirements, thus leaving only rich provinces in a position to supplement central state allocations and thus further to uneven investment levels across provinces. Finally, the methodology used for the commune-led process of identifying poor households, more often than not, has not rendered a comprehensive picture of poverty and its changes over the years. Program efforts thus have not reached many qualified beneficiaries (Do Kim Chung et al., 2015).

Although Vietnam has created a framework to deliver multi-sector programs, the decentralized state continues to come up short in promoting direct beneficiaries' participation, streamlining implementation documents, and decentralizing implementation to districts and communes while strengthening community accountability for poverty reduction performance.

3.5.3 Local Development

Among the six decentralization clusters, land management and foreign direct investment are the two with the greatest scope of decentralization; both exhibit only limited central control. Successive Land Laws between 1988 and 2013 have recognized the local state's extensive role in land management (Le Duc Thinh & Dao Trung Chinh, 2010).[8] However, loopholes in these legal frameworks for land management have opened up opportunities for local state officials to advance policies for private benefit. In FDI management, management decentralization has motivated provinces to improve local investment conditions and stimulated competition among them. A close look at the decentralized state apparatus in these two areas illustrates how a decentralized structure with limited central intervention may generate local state–citizen tension on the one hand and provincial fence-breaking on the other. Both cases shed light on the need to bolster transparency, accountability, and effective coordination in support of decentralized local development.

Land Management

In practice, almost every land management responsibility leaves local state officials leeway for interpretation. In the area of land use planning, for example, because Vietnam has not developed a legal framework to enshrine planning documents, it has become common for each new provincial leader in each term of office to revise and amend plans. Amendments more often than not benefit state officials who have the authority to adjust planning documents, officials at the implementation level, officials' family members, and patronage networks at the central and local levels. In the area of land acquisition and compensation, when the 2003 framework defined the conditions wherein the local state could acquire land for economic development purposes, there remained loopholes that enabled state officials in charge to re-interpret or revise the scope of land to

---

[8] By 2003, the state's responsibilities regarding land management had been defined to include promulgation of legal documents on management and use; fixing of administrative boundaries and maps and the management of related documents; surveys and classification; planning; allocation, leasing, acquisition, and conversion of use and purposes; registration of use rights; inventories and statistics; land-sector financial management; development of markets for land use rights; management of user rights and obligations; inspection and supervision of compliance with laws and handling of violations; response to complaints and denunciations of management and usage violations; managing land-related public service activities; and certification and validation of transactions (Le Duc Thinh & Dao Trung Chinh, 2010).

be acquired and the compensation scheme for acquisition (Le Duc Thinh, 2010).

As these practices suggest, the process of re-zoning agricultural and urban land for development purposes has not always been fair to local inhabitants. Under the state compensation price framework, land has been appropriated at consistently lower than market rates and then resold at a profit. Though various land laws outline procedures for land clearance and compensation, in practice local state officials do not always follow these procedures. The lack of integrity in land management has been a key reason for citizen petitions, noncompliance with land clearance, and outright protest.

The late-1990s case of the Thu Thiem Urban Development Project in Ho Chi Minh City illustrates how the provincial state has approached spatial planning, land clearance, and land compensation. While Prime Minister Võ Văn Kiệt approved the Thu Thiem Project in 1996, since then, the Ho Chi Minh City's People's Committee has reportedly adjusted the project's scope (*Thanh Niên*, May 4, 2018). In the course of project implementation, local residents questioned the legal basis for clearance of and compensation for the project parcel. Their specific grievances focused on low compensation prices in comparison with high resale prices and the arbitrary requisition of land areas believed not to fall under the original spatial planning scope. Local residents submitted petitions that challenged the People's Committee of Quarter 2, which was the administrative unit authorized by the Ho Chi Minh City's People' Committee to clear land. Petitioners also sought redress from the court after local authorities forcibly impounded or demolished their homes.

In 2018, Prime Minister Nguyễn Xuân Phúc assigned the Government Inspectorate to review the causes of the citizens' petitions. The Inspectorate concluded that an area of 4.3 hectares was located outside the project's spatial framework and was unlawfully requisitioned. This extra area had been added to the spatial plan by Ho Chi Minh City's Head Architect in 1998, who lacked authority over plan adjustment. The Government Inspectorate also pointed to the local state's violations of land clearance and compensation regulations. Local residents rejected these conclusions, insisting that the land area outside the original spatial plan was larger than the identified 4.3 hectares (Thông báo, 2018). It is worth noting that there was no legal review of plan adjustments over four terms of Ho Chi Minh City leadership, from 1996 to 2016.

The decade-long contention between the local state and local residents reflected emerging challenges to the management of decentralization frameworks in areas of both mandate and accountability. Fundamentally, the challenge is the fact that planning documents do not have sufficient legal status to compel agencies' implemention of them, while plan adjustments are not transparent. Furthermore, there is no mechanism to monitor land requisition or compensation procedures. Administrative petitioning is not an effective mechanism to address grievances, as state agencies have a tendency to protect one another at the expense of citizens' interests. Land management is exemplary of extensive management decentralization without institutionalized accountability mechanisms.

Foreign Direct Investment

While decentralized land management has affected local state–citizen relations, from the late 1990s onward decentralized FDI management in general and domestic investment in particular have precipitated competition among provinces in the process of attracting investment resources. This competition has taken various forms. While some provinces reorganized the local state apparatus to promote an enabling environment, some opted to adjust existing central regulations arbitrarily for local benefit. These cases reflect elements of "fence-breaking," that is, convenient reinterpretation or even outright breach of existing central regulations. These experiments took place in the context of tacit central support for innovation and increasingly strict control over violations deemed detrimental to central frameworks.

The very first innovation provinces adopted was to reduce bureaucratic red tape inherited from the era of central planning. To a large extent this initiative aligned with Resolution 38 of 1994, calling for ministries and provinces to simplify administrative procedures required of citizens and organizations. While Ho Chi Minh City was among the first to pilot simplified administrative procedures at the district level, the story of Binh Duong, one of Vietnam's earliest industrialized provinces, illustrates how a provincial state's innovation can stimulate an economic breakthrough.

The Binh Duong provincial leadership was methodical in "rolling out the red carpet" (*trải thảm đỏ*) to welcome foreign investors. From the start, the leadership prioritized systematic investment in infrastructure, transparency of investment decision making, and simplification of administrative procedures in areas of land management, business registration, investment, construction, inspection of businesses, and taxation. Binh Duong's approach to land clearance and compensation as of the 1990s was comparatively straightforward, offering market prices and ensuring employment for those who would lose their land. This innovation was based on local state authorities' interpretations and loopholes in legal documents. By 2012, Binh Duong successfully accommodated close to 2,100 FDI projects (with a value of USD $17.12 billion) out of 2,208 registered projects (with a total value of $17.49 billion). Binh Duong's popularity as an investment destination turned it into the third largest investment region in Vietnam (*Tin tức*, January 31, 2013). Seeing the success of this early industrializer, other provinces followed suit with improvements in their own investment environments by simplifying administrative procedures. Other successful cases include Da Nang in central Vietnam and Vinh Phuc in the Red River Delta.

Reducing investment-related bureaucratic red tape was not so simple, however. A study published in 2011 identified some seventy procedures. Requirements were under the jurisdiction of at least four line agencies: planning and investment, construction, natural resources and environment, and finance. In addition, certain FDI investment projects also required Ministry of Public Security and MOHA involvement (IFC et al., 2011). Success in simplifying investment procedures required strong provincial-level leadership to coordinate state agencies, use of information technology to facilitate sharing of sector plans, and a contact point to deliver services transparently. As it turned out, not all provinces were successful in developing a local state apparatus supportive of FDI.

Beyond initiatives for innovation and streamlined central regulatory frameworks, many provinces opted to offer potential investors preferential treatment. This treatment ranged from favorable land-rental agreements and tax exemptions to lax environmental impact assessment standards. One study of provinces' preferential schemes between 2001 and 2005 points out that 32 of Vietnam's 64 provinces violated central investment guidelines to attract FDI, undermining the fiscal position of the local and central state alike (Vu Thanh Tu Anh, Le Viet Thai, and Vo Tat Thang, 2007). At the same time, thirteen provinces have successfully generated revenue surpluses over the last decade (*CAFEF*, October 14, 2016).

The story of those provinces that have remained agricultural and cannot finance investment, however, is somewhat different. As discussed earlier, the central government easily approves provincial public investment proposals along with fiscal transfers for their implementation. SOEs under provincial jurisdiction have more often than not been investors and contractors on public investment projects, been awarded concessions and contracts on a noncompetitive basis, and received government-directed bank loans. There is apparently a symbiotic relationship between SOEs and the provincial states. SOEs rely on local governments for access to land and land-based resources, as land management falls under provincial jurisdiction. The local state, in turn, needs SOE projects in order to benefit from tax revenue their investments generate.

3.5.4 SOEs as a Driving Force for Change

The party-state leadership has considered SOEs to be overall drivers for change. Although there were differences in the emphasis on the role of the state sector during the Võ Văn Kiệt, Phan Văn Khải, and Nguyễn Tấn Dũng governments, the party-state leadership routinely adopted measures to strengthen the state sector. While calling for corporatizing small and medium-sized SOEs, party-state leaders also piloted new organizational models of state general corporations (SGCs) as early as the 1990s and state economic groups (SEGs) after 2000. Although in principle SGCs only focus on one key business and SEGs comprise groups of diverse businesses, in practice the distinction between the two has become blurred over the years.

In the wake of Vietnam's accession to the WTO, leaders have consolidated existing SGCs into highly diversified SEGs. In 2005 and 2006, eight SEGs were created; by 2011, that number rose to thirteen. SEGs retain traditional SOE privileges in accessing state-controlled resources, especially land, natural resources, development assistance credit, infrastructure investment, and public procurement. The VCP and the state also created conditions for SEGs to raise capital by allowing them to set up banking, insurance, and financial companies. They only report to the Prime Minister on issues such as current business activities; investment plans and the investment structure of their core and non-core business; capital mobilisation; bank, real estate, and stock market activities; and the form and level of cooperation among enterprises within each economic group (Vietnam Executive Leadership Program, 2012–2015). The central state uses industrial policies to support targeted SEGs, while SEGs play key roles in preparing sector strategies.

Despite extensive investment, however, SOEs of various types have not been efficiently managed. During the term of Prime Minister Nguyễn Tấn Dũng (2006–2016), the shortcomings of SEGs were revealed, as in the case of the Vietnam Shipbuilding Industry Group, Vinashin. Set up in 1996 with the aim of becoming one of the world's top shipbuilders, Vinashin rapidly expanded but incurred a debt of USD $4.5bn before defaulting in 2010 on $600 million in loans (*Financial Times*, March 27, 2012). The state-owned PetroVietnam, an oil and natural gas company, one of the three biggest SEGs in Vietnam, also reportedly suffered massive losses between 2008 and 2011 (*BBC News*, January 8, 2018).

Proponents of SOEs of various forms argue that their operation is not always aimed at profit or economic efficiency. Though SOEs attempt to maximize profits, they are also responsible for developing poor areas and supplying public utilities, activities which generate little profit. Proponents of SOEs also agree, however, that there is no excuse for an SOE to be incompetent. Economic pros and cons notwithstanding, from a political point of view the strengthening of the state sector in the economy amounts to the consolidation of the one-party state's economic and political power.

3.5.5 Regulation of the Private Sector

Even though the VCP and the central government have endorsed the development of the private sector (that is, private businesses and the household economic sector engaged in nonagricultural activities), in practice small and medium-sized enterprises are at a disadvantage as they are required to follow a similar set of regulatory requirements to larger firms, despite their smaller size and less complicated project scope. They have encountered difficulties in starting up, sustaining operations, and competing with the state and FDI sectors.

Over the past three decades, various governments have attempted to simplify administrative procedures for private businesses. The most successful area of administrative procedural reform has been enterprise entry registration, which was largely a joint effort between the MPI, the Ministry of Public Security, and the Bureau of Taxation to streamline entry registration requirements. According to statistics provided by the Federation of Trade and Industry Associations of Hanoi, the number of registered enterprises nationwide increased from 53,244 in 2000 to 349,300 by June 2008. In Hanoi, the number rose from 6,559 to 64,000. Small and medium-sized enterprises formed 93.95% of total enterprises and employed 50.13% of the labor pool. Despite such a tremendous increase in the number of registered enterprises, survival has remained a challenge for them post-registration, and the percentage of enterprises in actual operation decreased from 70.78% in 2000 to 65% by June 2008 (Vasavakul et al., 2009).

Nor has ease of enterprise entry registration always aligned with ease of doing business. Surveys conducted from 1990 to 2000 show that temporary tax exemptions in the start-up phase had a positive influence on long-run growth for non-household enterprises while initial credit support seemed to have benefitted rural firms. Overall, private enterprises that had SOEs as their main customers performed better (Hasen et al., 2009). Nonetheless, private firms reportedly have faced complicated administrative procedures related to land, credit, and market access, leading to exceptionally high overhead. For example, the processing times for land use certificates were at one point two hundred times longer for private firms than for SOEs (Tenev et al., 2003: 67). Access to credit was closely associated with connections to party, government, or SOEs. Market access was also easier for state-connected firms (Malesky & Taussig, 2008). There have been indications that citizens resort to paying informal fees to expedite paperwork. 22.71% of respondents to the Vietnamese Provincial Competitive Index's nationwide survey for 2008 admitted that they paid bribes to get procedures processed more quickly.

The General Bureau of Statistics indicated that as of January 1, 2013, Vietnam had 347,693 enterprises in operation, 96% of which were in the private sector. The private sector's contribution had increased from 22.9% of total investment capital in 2000 to 37.6% in 2013, yet this sector now shows signs of setback. In 2013, 9,818 private enterprises closed while 50,919 suspended operations, an increase over the previous year. While the number of new private enterprises increased in 2013, the volume of capital decreased when compared with 2012 (Phạm Thị Thu Hằng, 2014).

That successive attempts to address the administrative procedural burden on businesses have not brought about immediate results may be attributable to the structure of the *đổi mới* state apparatus. The *đổi mới* state consists of units with overlapping functions within and across sectors, an overlap that has fostered duplicate procedural requirements. Lack of coordination among sectors and between administrative levels has also created administrative bottlenecks.

3.6 Legitimacy of the *Đổi Mới* State and Its Growth Model

At one level, the decentralized state structure that has emerged in the era of *đổi mới* has been politically and economically inclusive, and as a result appears legitimate, at least from the perspective of the VCP and the state leadership.

Politically, the VCP leadership structure, especially its Central Committee, consists of representatives from different political institutions: the VCP itself, mass and professional organizations, the administrative state, the National Assembly, and the judicial branch. On the state side, both ministerial-level leaders and provincial party chiefs are members of the Central Committee. Of the Central Committee members endorsed at the Twelfth National Party Congress, 36% were provincial party chiefs. Within the state apparatus, management decentralization has granted both central ministries and provinces considerable authority over sector and territorial management. Since the official endorsement of *đổi mới*, it has become increasingly common practice for all legal documents to include a section on management decentralization. However, the VCP has centralized certain powers through the system of cadre rotation as a stepping-stone to leadership. Limited devolution of decision-making power has further motivated central and state agencies to adopt the "asking and giving" practice. Both cadre rotation and the "asking and giving" practice have given rise to patronage networks within the state apparatus. Political inclusion, patronage networks, and power dispersal, in turn, serve as bases for one-party state legitimacy at the leadership level.

Economically, the state has adopted a growth model based on a combination of centralized and decentralized accumulation and allocation. The central state – relying on revenue from tax collection, oil and gas sales, and borrowing – has allocated resources through the state budget in the form of recurrent expenditure for the VCP and the state apparatus, public investment, national target programs, and SOE investment. For the most part resources are distributed evenly, albeit thinly, across sectors and provinces. Provincial states accumulate capital through land management and domestic and foreign investment while also benefitting from central transfers. Liberal resource accumulation and central-local resource allocation have, to a large extent, legitimated the one-party state.

Despite economic benefits brought about by reforms, citizens from all walks of life have increasingly become critical of the symptoms and results of economic achievement, ranging from corruption and public debt to a decline in management quality across sectors. Since Vietnam came into open military conflict over the PRC's expansion in the South China Sea, citizens have linked state legitimacy with VCP and government policies toward China in general, and Chinese economic activities in Vietnam in particular. Citizens have attributed state ineffectiveness to the rise of "interest groups" within the VCP and the state apparatus, calling for increased accountability and for recognition of citizen rights to voice concerns and disagreements through public protests.

4 Accountability of the *Đổi Mới* State

The accountability mechanisms that have emerged since the era of *đổi mới* do not strictly follow any principle of institutional checks and balances. Crafted in an uncoordinated and piecemeal way since the mid-1990s, they have all nonetheless reflected attempts to limit specific "self-aggrandizing" tendencies on the part of the decentralized state apparatus, within state policy, and in the exercise of state power. Four types of accountability have each targeted their designated state structures: citizen, administrative, legal-consultative, and institutional.

Briefly, citizen accountability focuses on the promotion of local residents and their role in holding local authorities accountable. It is often known as basic-level or grassroots democracy (*dân chủ cơ sở*) accountability. Administrative accountability focuses within the state apparatus, especially between upper and lower echelons and between agency heads and subordinates. It can be seen in the introduction of performance measures, the control of the state regulatory role, inspections, and corruption prevention. Legal-consultative accountability focuses on accountability between state lawmakers and citizens. It can be seen in the mandatory collection of citizen input during the drafting of legal documents. Institutional accountability focuses on accountability between institutions and is evident through strengthening of elected bodies at the national and local levels to perform representative, legislative, and supervisory roles vis-à-vis the executive.

These accountability mechanisms have not been designed to promote a full-fledged system of institutional checks and balances, but were introduced largely in response to public criticism of state ineffectiveness and mass protests against abuses of state power over the years.

4.1 Protests in Thai Binh Province and Citizen Accountability

Under one-party rule, large-scale protests have been rare, largely as the result of a changing state structure that has constrained such political mobilization at the local level across the nation. Under state socialism, popular resistance took place mostly within the state structure, out of either cooperative or state-run production units, and the uniformity of the state socialist system made individually orchestrated acts of noncompliance powerful. In the era of *đổi mới*, the decentralized state structure has kept popular resistance contained to localities, which increasingly differ in their domestic concerns. The decentralized state structure has also had the effect of localizing state responses, making popular grievances "local" rather than "national."

The mass protests in Thai Binh in 1997 can be classified as serious given that Thai Binh is the revolutionary cradle of the VCP dating to the anticolonial period. The protests took place over several months, involved a large number of communes and districts, and unleashed public grievances upon local-level officials. The incident escalated out of a peaceful demonstration at the provincial office in May 1997 to demand that local officials be punished for "excessive" corruption. In June, following a lack of response to this initial protest, rural inhabitants across communes seized the offices of the Commune People's Committees, vandalized state property, and set fire to the houses of key local party and state officials. By the end of June, the protests and disturbances had spread to five out of seven districts. Demonstrators were reportedly supported by retired party, state, and army officials. The issues were unfair land distribution, unjustified fee collections, and misuse of local contributions by commune and district authorities on infrastructure. The Thai Binh incident has not been the only mass protest in Vietnam under *đổi mới*. Other small-scale local protests throughout the *đổi mới* era have focused on land grabbing and unfair compensation associated with infrastructure development projects, living and working conditions in factories, environmental concerns, and human rights violations triggered by religious restrictions and legal trials.

Benedict Kerkvliet (2014) observes that authorities are more tolerant of criticism of particular government policies or programs than of the government broadly; of particular non-senior officials than of top national leaders; of individual critics than large groups; and of protests by peasants and workers than by the middle class. The VCP and the government are less tolerant of what they perceive as "acts against the SRV." Carl Thayer (2014) identifies four groups targeted by the state's repressive measures since the first decade of the twenty-first century: political activists under the name Bloc 8406, Catholic Church-led land protesters, Zen Buddhist followers of Thích Nhất Hạnh, and ethnic minority activists in the Central Highlands.

The Thai Binh unrest and other public protests that unfolded during the first two decades after the official endorsement of *đổi mới* prompted the VCP, the government, and the National Assembly to issue guidelines to promote democracy in commune-level administration.[9] These moves signaled recognition of the need for greater accountability to the citizenry from local officials, while also clarifying boundaries for direct citizen engagement.

4.1.1 Basic-Level Democracy at the Commune Level

Basic-level, or grassroots, democracy frameworks (*dân chủ cơ sở*) endorse the fourfold co-governance principle that "people know, people discuss, people act, and people monitor" (*dân biết, dân bàn, dân làm, dân kiểm tra*). Commune-level authorities are required to disclose information about decisions directly affecting the community. Residents in turn participate in formulating locally funded projects, drafting village conventions, managing village internal affairs, supervising public-funded construction projects, and maintaining local security and social safety. Additionally, they are asked to comment on documents before local authorities promulgate them; and finally, they are involved in directly supervising selected government activities, judicial processes, and financial affairs. This "people monitor" principle is

---

[9] The notion of grassroots democracy was later extended to cover democracy in enterprises and each governmental unit.

channelled through the People's Inspectorate (*Ban thanh tra nhân dân*) and the Committee for Monitoring Public Infrastructure Investment (*Ban Giám sát đầu tư cộng đồng*) (Vasavakul, 2006 and 2012).

A 2012 small-scale survey of provincial VFF units, the main units responsible for the implementation of basic-level democracy in provinces, provides insight as to how "people know, people discuss, people act, and people monitor" works in practice.[10] The survey results show that the commune-level administration disclosed information only moderately; 61.8% of respondents from the VFF agreed that local authorities shared information on spending items drawn from local funds.

Regarding the "people discuss" principle, 76.5% of respondents confirmed that citizens took part in deciding the levels of popular contribution to public projects, but in other areas of decision making this consensus dropped below half. For example, only 47.1% agreed that commune-level governments had sought citizen opinions on activities that infringed on their rights, while 35.3% agreed that commune-level governments had sought opinions from citizens on master plans directly affecting their lives.

When asked about the "people act" principle in practice, only one-third of respondents confirmed that their province had such a policy, while around half stated that their province was in the process of piloting one. Likewise, the survey showed only a moderate incidence of the "people monitor" practice. Only 29.4% of the respondents totally agreed that the People's Inspectorate Units (PIU) in their locality performed monitoring work efficiently.

On another point, 20.6% agreed that citizens took part in monitoring local government responses to petitions and other problems arising in various localities. When asked about the overall role of the People's Inspectorate Unit at the commune level, between 38% and 50% rated its activities as having met requirements.

Among the four principles "the people know, the people discuss, the people act, and the people monitor," the "people monitor" seemed least realized. Overall, PIUs faced several challenges to their effectiveness: the existing decentralized structure, leadership, working procedures, finances, and capacity. Structurally, the scope of management decentralization to the commune-level administration had been limited, and as a result the scope of monitoring work done at this level by PIUs was correspondingly limited. Although the leadership selection process was from the bottom up, elected leaders had to be approved by commune party leaders. In communes where VFF leadership

---

[10] This survey was supported by the Committee for Democracy and Law at the central VFF office in Hanoi. About 70% of the provincial VFF offices responded to the survey.

was prestigious and the VFF was allowed some independence to choose PIU members, the PIU, too, tended to be self-directing. In many localities, on the other hand, when the PIU monitored projects receiving popular contributions, there was no analogous procedure for monitoring state-funded projects, nor was the unit involved in monitoring either projects run by private investors or ones that appropriate land for industrial zones. PIU finances imposed another constraint; each PIU received VND 2 million (approximately USD $100) per year, although in practice the budget allocated ranged from VND 1.5 to VND 3 million depending on the availability of funds from the commune-level administration budget. Finally, as members of the PIU were elected from a pool of hamlet-level heads, many qualified people were automatically left out. All these challenges were common to all PIUs across Vietnam's communes and wards (Vasavakul, 2012).

Overall, despite a good practice model, basic-level democracy frameworks have been selective regarding the information to be disclosed and the policy areas in which local inhabitants may participate. In addition, to implement basic-level democracy frameworks fully there is a need for additional work rules facilitating the various modes of popular participation. Furthermore, the implementation of basic-level democracy also requires strengthening the role of the VFF from the provincial to the local level. Given these constraints, in practice, the exercise of basic-level democracy varies across communes and provinces.

4.1.2 People's Audit

In addition to the PIU, the Committee for Monitoring Public Infrastructure (CMPI) is another basic-level institution specifically designed to engage citizens in monitoring public investment projects. According to a 2005 Prime Ministerial Decision, a commune's VFF is to set up the commune's CMPI upon the community's request. The CMPI audits both state and community-funded projects to evaluate the relevance of investment decisions and to assess their compliance with existing regulations on land management, construction, and environment as well as implementation progress. Although the CMPI is not originally a component of the basic-level democracy framework, its monitoring function overlaps that of the PIU.

During its first few years, Decision 80 and the commune-level CMPI were not widely implemented, and even at that only on small-scale projects with local contributions, not projects funded in the state budget. A close look at communes that carried out people's auditing through the CMPI, nonetheless, indicates that a mature community monitoring system helped reduce waste and corruption risks. For example, according to a commune in Bac Ninh province bordering Hanoi, for the period from January 2006 to April 2009, the local CMPI conducted monitoring work on eight infrastructure projects funded by both the state budget and popular contributions. The projects included a two-story school building, a hamlet cultural house, a cement road through a hamlet, and a VFF office at the commune level. The size of the planned investment capital was between VND 540 million and 4.3 billion. For these projects CMPI were successful in detecting collusion between companies and material suppliers during implementation, and commune records show that the monitoring work helped save between 3% and 57.7% of the planned budget.[11]

Despite the CMPI being a proven accountability mechanism, technical requirements and capacity constraints on locally recruited CMPI members have also proved to be a challenge. However, the central government's mandate for a people's audit of local infrastructure components managed by the commune-level administration has sustained the CMPI framework. Legally, the CMPIs and the PIUs are two separate entities, and many localities keep them that way. Given the similar monitoring functions of the PIU, however, many others have merged the two bodies to concentrate resources better. In the final analysis, the expansion of the CMPI has had the effect of reinforcing the "people monitor" principle of grassroots democracy.

4.2 Administrative Accountability

Within the state apparatus, successive governments and central state agencies have created and strengthened state mechanisms for holding agencies accountable. Within the framework of the PAR-MP, the Ministry of Home Affairs (MOHA) standardized one-stop shop mechanisms to provide administrative procedural services at the central, provincial, district, and commune levels. The MOHA also developed the Public Administration Reform Index (PAR Index) to track PAR implementation and results. Meanwhile, the Vietnam Inspectorate embarked on reform in its sector for stronger inspection of state agencies' legal compliance and more effective frameworks for citizen complaints and denunciation. Corruption-busting was another agenda that emerged as early as the 1990s with the purpose of curbing the abuse of state positions.

These initiatives have served the "path-breaking" purpose of forcing reorganization of state agencies' inner workings, standardizing performance, and bringing greater integrity to the state system. In the process they have also helped undercut developing patronage networks within the state structure.

---

[11] Information gathered from a field trip arranged by the Office of the National Steering Committee for Anti-Corruption in 2007.

4.2.1 Administrative Service Delivery through One-Stop Shops

Attempts to simplify administrative procedures were made through mechanisms known as "one-door/one-stop" (*một cửa một dấu*), generally known in English as one-stop shops (OSS). Between 2003 and 2007, the MOHA officially introduced and tested the OSS as a means to deliver multiple administrative services to citizens in a single place. The one-stop shop was designed to receive applications, transfer application materials to line units for processing, and return results directly to applicants. Each OSS was required to adhere to a set of standard service delivery practices, such as publishing requirements, maintaining fee-transparency, and returning results punctually. In 2007, the MOHA began to use the OSS to channel administrative procedures handled by various government sectors and administrative levels. The designation "inter-sector one-stop shop" thus referred to delivery of procedures handled by multiple sectors while "inter-level one-stop shop" referred to the OSS delivering procedures handled by various administrative levels. Given that all types of OSS separated citizens from the officials who handled their requests, they were expected to help curtail abuses of power. It was also believed that the "one-door" principle would help restructure the internal work processes of state agencies (Vasavakul et al., 2009).

Results from a small-scale survey conducted in 2012 provide a useful first glimpse of the degree to which the OSS mechanism had developed in Vietnam's provinces. First and foremost, the survey shows that the OSS had become institutionalized. Over three-quarters of the respondents (85.7%) confirmed that the majority of administrative procedures were carried out through an OSS. Second, Vietnam's provinces were developing both inter-sector and inter-level OSS (62% and 43% of provinces, respectively). Third, the survey results do indicate problems with the operational quality of some OSS. Less than half of the respondents (43%) answered that their province had applied information technology to the OSS and only a third (33.3%) answered that their province had surveyed customer satisfaction (Vasavakul, 2012).[12]

Overall, there have remained differences among provinces in their development of inter-sector and inter-level OSS. Modest development levels are not surprising given that both inter-sector and inter-level OSS require responsible line agencies and administrative echelons to commit to redefining relevant work processes. Furthermore, certain inter-sector OSS mechanisms require coordination between provincial line agencies and vertically organized state

---

[12] The survey form was sent to the provincial DOHA. Approximately half of the provinces answered the survey.

agencies located in given localities but managed by central ministries, a process requiring both central and provincial leadership commitment.

4.2.2 Public Administration Reform Index and Satisfaction Index for Administrative Services

Although the MOHA, under the stipulations of PAR-MPs (2001–2010 and 2011–2020), has been delegated responsibility as the lead agency responsible for PAR, it has met with challenges in tracking PAR implementation by ministries and provinces. To a large extent, these challenges have stemmed from the fact that being one among equals, MOHA does not have full authority to enforce PAR implementation and reporting. During the period of the 2001–2010 PAR-MP, PAR implementation was uneven across ministries and provinces and PAR reporting was intermittent and unsystematic.

In 2012, the MOHA developed two separate systems to measure the implementation of the PAR-MP and the performance of ministries and provinces: the PAR Index (*chỉ số cải cách hành chính*) and the Satisfaction Index for Public Administration Services or SIPAS (*chỉ số hài lòng về sự phục vụ hành chính*). The overall purpose of the PAR Index is to hold ministries and provinces accountable in implementing the required reform measures. The PAR Index asks ministries to self-assess their implementation of key PAR measures: leadership in PAR, institutional restructuring, procedural streamlining, reorganization, improved professional capacity, financial reform, and administrative modernization. Questions for the provinces are similar, with an additional item gauging commitment to the development of the OSS (Vasavakul, 2012). Self-assessment results from ministries and provinces are jointly reviewed by both self-assessors and MOHA officials. The objective of SIPAS is to measure the satisfaction of citizens and organizations regarding administrative services delivered by state agencies. Each state agency designs its own SIPAS using the four following service areas: citizen access to services, simplicity of administrative procedures, quality of services, and overall work results of state agencies. To supplement provincial assessment, the MOHA also conducts nation-wide surveys in collaboration with the VFF and the Association of Vietnam's Veterans. Both PAR Index and SIPAS have been supported by the National Steering Committee for Public Administration Reform revived in 2016 and led by a deputy Prime Minister.

According to the 2017 results published by the MOHA, twelve ministries and ministerial-level agencies scored over 80/100 and seven ministries and ministerial-level agencies scored lower than 80/100. The State Bank of Vietnam performed the best. Ministries that scored lower than 80/100 were the Ministries of Culture, Sports, and Tourism; Transportation; the Government Inspectorate; Construction; Planning and Investment; Education and Training; Health, and the Committee for Ethnic Minorities. The 2017 PAR Index indicates that provinces implemented PAR better than in 2016. Of the 63 provinces, Quang Ninh performed the best followed by Hanoi, Dong Nai, Da Nang, and Hai Phong (Bộ Nội vụ, 2018).

The results of the 2017 SIPAS survey of over 30,000 service users jointly conducted by the MOHA, the VFF, and the Association of Vietnam's Veterans shed light on administrative delivery at the provincial level. They show that around 92% of state agencies delivered administrative services to citizens as scheduled while around 2.4% delivered the services earlier than scheduled and 6% missed deadlines. Around 3.4% of service users reported that state officials intentionally caused difficulties in the process and close to 2% reported that officials requested informal payment. Although some 78% of respondents made only 1–2 visits to complete required administrative procedures, 17% made 3–4 visits and 2.4% made seven visits. The number of visits indicates that the inter-level and inter-sector OSS mechanisms are not yet functioning. Asked to rate their satisfaction with administrative service delivery, over a quarter of the respondents were satisfied with services and officials, and three-quarters were satisfied with availability of services and feedback channels (Bộ Nội vụ et al., 2018).

Both PAR Index and SIPAS are new accountability mechanisms for PAR implementation and performance management. Given that the PAR Index uses implementation as the measurement standard, it has compelled ministries and provinces to move towards change within the central framework. SIPAS has reminded state agencies of the need to link PAR implementation with certain citizen-oriented outcomes.

4.2.3 Inspection

Inspection, as a mechanism of ensuring the accountability of sub-units to their head agency, has had a long history in Vietnam, such that today every ministry and province has its own inspection unit. A given inspectorate's key function is to review the implementation of policies and laws and the discharge of agency, organizational, and individual responsibilities within the purview of the corresponding administrative authority. An inspectorate's objective is to detect and prevent legal violations and to discover managerial, policy, and legal loopholes. Inspection work may be carried out according to an annual schedule, upon order of the head of agency, or in response to citizen petitions and denunciations. In addition, inspectorates also process complaints and allegations of wrongdoing and assist the heads of relevant agencies in reviewing and resolving such allegations. Within the framework of the 2005 and subsequent Anti-Corruption Laws, the Inspectorate inspects the implementation of the Anti-Corruption Law, maintains a national database on preventing and combating corruption, provides assistance to the government in reporting anticorruption efforts to the National Assembly, and verifies public officials' assets and incomes. Given its mandate, the inspectorate sector is in a crucial position to strengthen the accountability of subunits to agency heads, accountability of the state agency to citizens, and accountability of state agencies generally in implementing anticorruption measures (Davidsen et al., 2007).

There are challenges in the use of inspections to hold state agencies accountable, however. In Vietnam, inspection units are attached to state agencies and placed under the leadership of agency heads. The use of inspections thus depends upon the will and commitment of the agency head. Additionally, agency heads are not obliged to accept a given inspectorate's findings, and even when they do the units being inspected may negotiate levels of both compliance and penalty. While some 80% of petitions submitted to the Inspectorate at different levels by citizens are related to administrative deliberations on land, the cases are handled slowly. Citizens are reportedly transferred repeatedly between state agencies and administrative levels without concrete results, leading to speculations as to a "corruption rope" (*đường dây tham nhũng*) within the state apparatus.[13] Overall, despite reform efforts, the inspectorate system can only partially perform its role as an accountability institution.

4.2.4 Anticorruption Institutions as Accountability Institutions

Vietnam's anticorruption efforts began in the early 1990s and were codified in the 1998 Ordinance on Anti-Corruption, the 2005 Law on Anti-Corruption, and subsequent revised laws. Drivers included concerns over illegal economic activities at the provincial levels and signs of state property theft in the 1990s, the Thai Binh protest in 1997, and Vietnam's commitment to the United Nations Convention on Anti-Corruption.

Vietnam's anticorruption frameworks have been explicit on who is to be held accountable for corrupt practices. The 1998 framework held "persons in state positions and with authority" (*người có chức vụ, quyền hạn*) accountable. The 2005 framework, nonetheless, shifted responsibility to hold agency heads specifically accountable when corrupt acts occurred in their agencies

---

[13] Interviews with petitioners in 2016–2017.

(Vasavakul, 2003b and 2008). Under Prime Minister Nguyễn Tấn Dũng, the National Steering Committee and its Permanent Office focused on petty corruption in state management across sectors.

However, relying on state anticorruption agencies as accountability agencies posed challenges. First, anticorruption steering tasks became dispersed across multiple jurisdictions; although there is no legal mandate to set up steering committees at the central ministerial and provincial levels, in 2007, the same year the National Steering Committee was set up, more than twenty central ministries and provinces reportedly undertook to do so (Davidsen et al., 2007). Furthermore, the 2005 Law to hold agency heads accountable for corruption within their agencies demotivated leadership at various levels from reporting actual wrongdoing. In the end, few of the actual corruption cases were reported by heads of state agencies; rather, corrupt practices were for the most part made public by the press, citizen complaints, or mass protests.

In light of the VCP's anticorruption drive during the term of General Secretary Nguyễn Phú Trọng (2011–2016 and 2016–present), the VCP transferred leadership of the National Anti-Corruption Steering Committee from the Prime Minister to the Politburo chaired by the General Secretary himself in 2013. General Secretary Nguyễn Phú Trọng has since been active in tackling grand corruption cases by holding VCP leaders *cum* state officials directly accountable for corruption, especially on cases that generated losses of state property. PetroVietnam Oil and Natural Gas Company, an SEG that incurred massive losses between 2008 and 2011, presents one landmark case, in which former General Director Đinh La Thăng, a Politburo member and Ho Chi Minh City Party Secretary, was held accountable when a 90% majority of the Party's Central Committee voted to remove him from his party positions in 2017 (*BBC News*, January 8, 2018). Trọng's anticorruption drives, if successful, could undermine various patronage networks in the VCP and the state apparatus.

4.2.5 Administrative Accountability in Official Discourse

While the effects of the drive for administrative accountability remain to be seen, the mechanisms developed represent significant changes in official discourse. The state apparatus developed under central planning was not one designed to "serve" the public. The newly introduced mechanisms focus on the notions of public service, public integrity, and satisfaction of citizens *cum* customers, all of which are designed to restrain the use of state power. They also have had the effect of restructuring the state's inner workings and standardizing its performance. Beyond this, the mechanisms put in place have facilitated an ongoing public discussion about how best to promote accountability and what standards might be used to assess it.

4.3 Accountability in the Drafting of Legal Documents

Vietnam's law on the promulgation of legal documents, also known as the "Law on Laws," has contributed to the development of accountability in legal drafting. The Law on Laws requires that lawmaking committees incorporate public consultation in their process and that public input be considered and used. The call for public consultation has had the effect of creating space for non-state actors to voice their concerns while balancing the executive-driven legal drafting process.

Vietnam has a complex structure of popular organizations, ranging from mass organizations and professional organizations inherited from the socialist period to issue-oriented popular organizations known as international non-governmental organizations (INGOs), and Vietnamese non-governmental organizations (VNGOs). The VFF and mass organizations, given their political status and their function as links between the VCP and their members, are procedurally consulted on draft legal documents. Prime Minister Phan Văn Khải's Decision 22/2002/QD-TTg of 2002 granted the Vietnam Union of Sciences and Technology (VUSTA) the mandate to conduct consultancy (*tư vấn*), appraisal (*phản biện*), and social evaluation (*giám định xã hội*), necessary for the lawmaking process. VUSTA also serves as a channel for small NGOs with practical experience at local levels to have access to legal drafters (CODE et al., 2008). The Vietnam Chamber of Commerce and Industry, an umbrella organization for businesses, is also active either in its capacity as a member of a Drafting Committee or as a reviewer (Vasavakul & Bui The Cuong, 2008). INGOs and VNGOs have introduced and institutionalized the practices of "lobbying" (*vận động hành lang*) or "policy advocacy" (*vận động chính sách*) as means to campaign for particular socioeconomic and political issues (CODE et al., 2008). INGOs and VNGOs have tended to work directly with either the drafting committees or National Assembly committees.

Although civic organizations of various types are able to convey their concerns to law makers, hurdles remain. Whether and how different civic organizations of various types have collected input from their members remains a question. There are also challenges around the timely disclosure of drafting documents and the process of consultation. The Provincial Competitive Index survey results for 2013 show that 82% of businesses surveyed had not offered any comments on draft legislation and policies, the main reasons being limited access to documents and limited time. In frequent cases the public consultation process did not include any impact assessment or report on the use of public input (Phạm Thị Thu Hằng, 2014). Obviously, to hold legal drafters accountable requires both timely disclosure of information and established channels for member participation.

There are indications that civic organizations are more successful when they rely on formal and informal networks in advocating for changes either in policy or in draft legal documents (Kerkvliet, Heng, & Koh, 2003; Wells-Dang, 2012). For example, in the 1990s, a coalition of professional associations, research organizations, and local communities, with support from a senior VCP member, joined forces to remove the Ministry of Culture's restrictions on cultural practices related to the veneration of Vietnam's Holy Mother (*thờ mẫu*), practices later recognized by UNESCO as an intangible World Cultural Heritage (Vasavakul, 2003a). In 2018, the public objected to a draft law on Special Economic Zones that would authorize a 99-year land concession to foreign investors on the basis put forward that the law would enhance opportunities for China's economic and territorial control within Vietnam. The late President Trần Đại Quang reportedly supported this line of thinking along with the delay of the bill's approval. In this case, the National Assembly decided to postpone review and passage of the draft law. Overall, there are indications that public consultation and feedback work as accountability mechanisms to balance executive-driven law and policy formulation when opinion is jointly supported by a wide range of stakeholders, from VCP leaders and state officials to technocrats, intellectuals, civic organizations, and citizens.

4.4 Institutional Accountability

In the era of *đổi mới,* Vietnam's National Assembly adopted landmark practices that qualified it as an accountability institution, trending away from being a mere "rubber stamp" organization. During the Eighth National Assembly (1987–1992), deputies proposed that Võ Văn Kiệt stand for Prime Minister against Đỗ Mười. Although Võ Văn Kiệt was not elected, the practice of proposing a second candidate itself was a break with prior political tradition. In 1989, the Assembly introduced a three-option voting system of "agree," "disagree," and "no vote." The abstention option justified disagreement while providing a milder tone than the more explicit "disagree." In 1991, the Assembly introduced sessions reserved for questioning ministers (*chất vấn*), a practice later institutionalized.

Under the chairmanship of Nông Đức Mạnh, the Ninth and Tenth National Assemblies (1992–1997, 1997–2002) were increasingly engaged in law making and monitoring through questioning sessions. In 1998, it institutionalized the broadcast of senior leaders' questioning sessions despite objections from party and state leadership circles. This consolidation had the effect of strengthening the Assembly's monitoring role. In 2001, the Law on the National Assembly was revised, giving the National Assembly the authority to conduct votes of confidence on senior state officials appointed or approved by the Assembly. During the Twelfth National Assembly (2007–2011), the Committee for Judicial Affairs was set up as a separate entity from the Committee for Laws, showing commitment to judicial affairs and anticorruption. These landmark 1990s policy introductions, especially the authority to vet and approve cabinet nominations, to question state officials, and to call votes of confidence, have increasingly allowed the National Assembly to communicate expectations and standards to state officials (Huy Đức, 2012; Văn phòng Quốc hội, 2016).

However, the National Assembly still faces challenges to its role as an institution of public accountability. VCP members form a major component of the National Assembly. The National Assembly chair is a Politburo member while most of the heads of National Assembly committees are in the VCP's Central Committee. More than 90% of the Assembly's deputies are members of the VCP. Within the National Assembly's structure the Assembly's Standing Committee has monopolized decision making and overshadowed the role of individual deputies. In terms of legislation, as discussed earlier, state agencies continue to play the key role in drafting laws. Laws the National Assembly passes also need to be elaborated upon by government decrees and ministerial circulars. The National Assembly supervisory role, while increasing, still does not cover all aspects of state management and public programs.

The provincial People's Councils are faced with the same challenges. VCP leaders hold key positions, and the provincial party chief often assumes the role of the chair of the People's Council while VCP, state, and mass organization officials form a major component of the Council's members. The Provincial People's Council's legal review work has largely focused on whether legal codes and documents align with national law. Monitoring work, mostly through small-scale surveys and questioning, is limited to the implementation of policies approved or endorsed in People's Council resolutions, not the effectiveness and efficiency of those policies or their performance in local areas (Vasavakul et al., 2009a).

Despite constraints on legislative and representative roles, elected bodies at the national and provincial levels have served well as forums for open debate on state plans and performance. Their monitoring role, mostly through questioning sessions and only incrementally, has also inculcated a culture of answerability in state officials. The recent Law on the Supervisory Activities of the National Assembly and the People's Councils, passed in 2015, has the potential to expand and strengthen the monitoring role of elected bodies and foster their ability to hold state officials accountable.

4.5 Accountability and the Decentralized State

Along with citizens, the VCP and various governments have devised accountability networks to curb the self-aggrandizing tendency of the state apparatus, state policy, and state power. These mechanisms are designed to redirect the course of state-building by promoting citizen participation, good practices in state management, integrity, and answerability. These mechanisms redefine horizontal relationships between citizens and the state, vertical relationships within the state apparatus, and cross-institutional relationships among political institutions under the one-party regime. The accountability mechanisms that developed under *đổi mới* do not neatly fit the check-and-balance model whereby the executive, legislative, and judiciary branches form a horizontal accountability relationship.

Nonetheless, within the context of administrative decentralization, there are indications that the ability of the central state and citizens to hold the provincial state accountable remains modest. While Resolution no. 8 (2004) and additional frameworks associated with the 2015 Law on Local Government have expanded provincial-level state functions, central state agencies have not developed corresponding frameworks to keep such newly empowered provincial states in check. There have likewise been few channels for citizens to control the performance of the local state given limitations of the PIUs, the CMIPs, and People's Councils as well as limited reach of civic organizations in Vietnam's provinces. All these gaps are potentially detrimental to decentralization efforts.

Two incidents that took place in 2016–2017 elucidate the problematic accountability of the decentralized one-party state. The first incident was a mass fish death along Vietnam's central coastal provinces that resulted from toxic chemical discharges from a foreign-owned steel plant in Ha Tinh province. The second was the handling of pedestrian walkway violations in Hanoi and Ho Chi Minh City. These cases shed light on the interplay between citizen, administrative, legal drafting, and institutional accountability.

The marine die-off along more than 200 kilometers (124 miles) of shoreline in April 2016 was attributed to the use of lethal chemicals by Hung Nghiep

Formosa Ha Tinh Steel Company in Ha Tinh province. In late June, the company admitted its mistake and agreed to pay USD $500 million in compensation. The incident highlights challenges in enforcing administrative, citizen, and institutional accountability in the process of preparing environmental impact assessment, in monitoring and enforcing environmental protection measures, and in handling emerging environmental problems. All these functions help characterize accountability within the state apparatus, among political institutions, and between the state and its citizens regarding environmental protection.

That the Ha Tinh People's Committee signed the FDI agreement with Hung Nghiep Formosa Ha Tinh Steel Company (under the backing of Formosa Plastic Group) to develop the steel plant in Ha Tinh makes the Ha Tinh People's Committee the key state agency responsible for the project's execution. Procedurally, Vietnam's legal documents on environment have required state agencies and foreign investors to conduct environmental impact assessments and consult with local residents on potential environmental impacts and protection measures prior to any project approval. The marine disaster suggests that there were some weaknesses in implementing these legal requirements among local and central state officials as well as foreign investors. While monitoring and enforcement of environmental protection fell to the responsibility of the Ha Tinh provincial agencies, the marine disaster indicates the provincial state's limited capacity to track Formosa Ha Tinh Steel Company's compliance consistently or accurately. Given that the project was an FDI project, there was no readily available channel through which civic organizations or local residents might involve themselves in monitoring environmental protection within the basic democratic framework.

The accountability role of the central state in these events was ambiguous given the context of management decentralization. Central state agencies practiced compliance monitoring in principle if mostly through reporting from the local state. Although the Ha Tinh incident took place in early April, it was not until early May that Prime Minister Nguyễn Xuân Phúc appointed a joint team from several ministries to investigate the disaster. Official statements at the beginning did not link the incident with Formosa Steel Company, surmising instead the possibility of naturally occurring toxic algae blooms. The Ministry of Natural Resources and Environment, given its mandate over the environment, took the lead as the government voice in publicly clarifying the situation. Actions from other central agencies were mostly practical, ranging from the demarcation of safe and unsafe maritime zones for fisheries to controlling the sale of contaminated marine contraband, and supporting the livelihoods of local inhabitants affected by the incident. Vietnam's National Assembly was not active during the marine disaster, as its final session had ended.

Initial responses came mostly from citizens. In May, local residents formed barricades along main highways in reaction to the embargo on suspicious seafood products. Citizens in Hanoi and Ho Chi Minh City staged protests to demand accountability. Their discontent was precipitated by the company's seeming insensitivity to the effects of the disaster as well as Ha Tinh's liberal terms and conditions for the project, especially regarding land rental. To a large extent, discontent was also triggered by perceived connections between mainland Chinese companies and Formosa Steel Company.

Within the context of Vietnam's decentralization framework, local and central state agencies as well as citizens are able to involve themselves in environmental protection. However, it is not uncommon for poor provinces such as Ha Tinh to favor FDI and perhaps overlook too readily the need to enforce regulatory investor compliance. Systematic enforcement of environmental safeguards is not solely up to the province; central state agencies, the National Assembly, and even the Ha Tinh People's Council also have responsibilities for clarifying legal requirements and holding the provincial state and investors accountable. Though technocrats and citizens were active during the incident, had they been involved in tracking legal loopholes and continually involved in monitoring, their efforts would have buttressed local state agency accountability. The mass fish death incident indicates accountability gaps within the state apparatus and in the role of society in holding local state officials accountable.

To a large extent the marine disaster strengthened the role of the central state between 2016 and 2018. The central state supported the livelihoods of citizens in the provinces affected by the marine disaster, ensured the safety of sea products on the market, monitored sea water toxicity and its impact in the region, and enforced the company's compliance with environmental protection measures going forward. Additionally, the Ministry of Natural Resources and Environment reportedly initiated a review of environmental protection at key FDI sites (*Người Lao Động*, May 17, 2018). The National Assembly, for its part, became more active in requesting reports on FDI projects' on-site operation.

In another incident, a local state's handling of pedestrian walkway violations also sheds light on accountability and its challenges in the context of management decentralization. In 2017, Hanoi and Ho Chi Minh municipalities launched drives dedicated to "returning pedestrian walkways to pedestrians." This goal involved removing obstacles erected by local residents on public walkways, such as motorcycle ramps, illegal parking, and street markets.

Despite commitments from both municipalities, violations did not disappear; motorcycle ramps were quickly re-erected, pedestrian walkways remained jammed with motorcycles, and street vendors returned. The incidents exposed a lack of clarity about urban planning policy regarding the rights of pedestrians and vendors. While responsible officials carried out implementation, they did not consistently enforce it. Inconsistent implementation raised questions about relations between municipal officials and lower echelons responsible for implementation. It also raised concern about the leadership of local party committees as well as the relationship between local party-state officials and law enforcement agencies, which were directly under the Ministry of Public Security. In addition, the drives indicated that the principles of grassroots democracy were not used to engage local residents and involve vendors in discussing the pros and cons of the campaign, acting on solutions, and monitoring results. Nor was there a systematic involvement of elected deputies at the local level during the campaign.

The accountability crises revealed in the mass fish death and the municipal walkway policy are not exhaustive, yet they reflect challenges resulting from an incomplete accountability project that has left out the enforcement of authority relations within the state apparatus, checks and balances among political institutions, and active civic engagement.

5 Regime Change and Legitimacy from a Comparative Perspective

Regime change in Vietnam during *đổi mới* has involved a transition from plan to market, state-building, and the development of accountability mechanisms. The transition process has had three interrelated movements. First, the transition from central planning originated within the state socialist structure and was driven by commercialized interests of elites and masses alike. The VCP, in response to the historical crisis of reunification, put forth frameworks that supported a change process. The results of change further justified and propelled the *đổi mới* agenda, culminating in the abolition of the centrally planned system. Second, the process of transition from central planning undermined the power of the central state as provinces mobilized and accumulated resources based on horizontal networking and the bypassing of the traditional central planning hierarchy. Third, the disintegration of central planning amounted to the disintegration of the political power of the central state. The interplay between economic transition and state power served as the foundation for the regime change. The second process of regime change, post–central-planning state-building, was marked by ongoing negotiations over the role of the state in the economy as well as over authority relations between central and local state agencies grown enmeshed in commercialized interests. Economically, the transition resulted in the institutionalization of a market-oriented, multi-sector economy with the state economic sector in the lead. Politically, *đổi mới* created a decentralized state structure with divisions of management authority among central and sub-national state units. State power was shared between central and provincial state agencies with small-scale decentralization from the province to district and commune levels.There have been attempts to curb the decentralized state's self-aggrandizing tendencies, the third process of regime change. To a considerable extent, the *đổi mới* state's accountability project addressed the three aspects of accountability: "upward," as when a subordinate performs according to standards assigned by a superior; "horizontal," when two agencies of equal authority abide by agreed-upon standards; and "vertical," as when a government is responsible to its citizens according to a constitution. By 2016, thirty years after the official launch of *đổi mới*, Vietnam's one-party state had substantially departed from that of the central planning period to become largely what it is today.

The *đổi mới* growth model has sustained regime legitimacy at the leadership level. Central state agencies, long responsible for national and long-term socio-economic development goals, now derive their economic power not only from foreign aid, accumulation in agriculture, and taxes from SOEs as in the central planning era, but also from foreign investment projects, import and export duties, and resource extraction, especially oil. Under central planning, the central state's relationship with local governments was based on allocations of targets and production inputs according to central plans. In the era of *đổi mới*, the central state's leverage has been shifted to allocating FDI projects, support for recurrent expenditures by the state apparatus and other political institutions, SOE investment, and the transfer of state resources for public investment and national target programs run sub-nationally. Central transfers to rich and poor provinces alike have not only stimulated local development but also sustained political support from provincial party and state officials. In the era of *đổi mới*, provinces have been granted more decentralized authority, ranging from planning and budgeting to land, SOE, service-delivery, and personnel management. Provinces have, however, adopted the practice of "asking and giving" to bypass decentralization framework constraints. This practice has given rise to patronage networks based on state institutions or territories. The patterns of resource allocation underlying the *đổi mới* growth model have accommodated central and sub-national state elites across sectors and levels, helping shore up the legitimacy of the *đổi mới* state in the eyes of the state elite.

Equally important to regime legitimacy at the leadership level is the political mobility pervading the VCP structure. Given the "partification of the state" inherited from the central planning period, the VCP has continued to dominate the political landscape. Key party members assume key central and local state positions and thus are positioned to benefit, directly or indirectly, from state policy implementation and the exercise of state power. The VCP cadre rotation mechanism, since its institutionalization in the late 1990s, has sustained vertical ties between central and local party levels. It has also opened up opportunities for central VCP leaders to integrate prominent local-level cadres as well as social connections within the VCP structure. Hence, central leaders up for promotion are rotated to the provincial level while successful and well-connected provincial leaders are now promoted to national-level positions. This political mobility within the VCP structure, as it intertwines with mobility within the state structure, has also helped reinforce one-party state legitimacy among party and state elites.

The combination of sustained economic growth, expansion of political space, accountability, and tolerance of small-scale public protests has been another factor in strengthening regime–society legitimization. Undoubtedly, Vietnamese society has benefitted from economic change brought about by *đổi mới*: Vietnam passed the USD $1,000 threshold of a lower-middle-income country in 2008, and *per capita* GDP has increased to a record USD $2,343 in 2017. Politically, the VCP and different governments have expanded channels for popular participation, ranging from the promotion of the principle that "the people know, the people discuss, the people act, and the people monitor" and the expansion of space in the political apparatus for newly emerging NGOs to strengthening the supervisory role of elected bodies. Overall, the *đổi mới* decentralized state has become more "customer-oriented," being held accountable on the basis of citizen satisfaction. Although the VCP still controls mass mobilization through the VFF and mass organizations, citizen groups are able to conduct issue-oriented political mobilization and orchestrate collective action through informal networking. The VCP and the central state have so far tolerated small-scale protests while remaining wary of perceived "hostile forces" deemed to threaten regime stability.

Nonetheless, despite growth and participation as the basis of legitimacy, the *đổi mới* state is not without constraints. While the decentralized structure of the state and its growth model has sustained the one-party regime, it has also fostered fragmentation and dispersal of state power as well as opportunities for abuse of power. Hence, the overall perception of state ineffectiveness and corruption across management sectors and levels. Accountability mechanisms are not fully independent from the VCP and the state structure, while the use of accountability mechanisms is more often than not politically motivated, either by internal party conflicts or in response to outright protests. Systemic corruption, chronic state ineffectiveness, and the selective use of accountability, whether real or only perceived, incrementally erode public confidence in the party-state leadership in particular and regime legitimacy in the eyes of society in general.

In the years to come, it seems that the Leninist regime in Vietnam will be faced with two main political options: to creatively adapt socialism to new conditions, or to follow models found in other developing countries. The first option is to retain the country's decentralized state structure while strengthening centralized supervision as well as local accountability in various forms. This option will additionally require the VCP and the government to rethink Vietnam's growth model, basing it on a different pattern of resource mobilization and allocation that emphasizes the private sector as a growth driver as well as public investment in social infrastructure and welfare. The option of reforming and strengthening the decentralized state structure could be justified by the fact that the decentralized *đổi mới* state largely originated in provincial-level dynamics during the transition period in the 1980s and the redefinition of central–local state authority relations in the subsequent decades. For the second option, that is, to follow models that exist in other countries, Vietnam may learn from successful practices in early industrializing countries. For example, there is no shortage of writings by foreign scholars on how Vietnam may learn from the developmental state model in the East Asian experience. Somewhat different from the decentralized *đổi mới* model, East Asian experiences highlight the need for a cohesive centralized and autonomous central state apparatus. Vietnamese advocates who have adopted this option have emphasized the detrimental effects of provincialism and suggested the need for state restructuring in the form of some kind of recentralization.

As a matter of fact, there have been some moves toward restructuring the *đổi mới* state during the Twelfth Congress (2016–present). The Sixth Plenum of the Central Committee that met in October 2017 endorsed the reorganization of the political structure, including the VCP, central and provincial state agencies, and mass organizations, with the potential effect of undercutting existing patronage networks. In 2018, the Eighth Plenum of the Central Committee and the National Assembly confirmed General Secretary Nguyễn Phú Trọng as the President of the SRV – meaning he will hold both offices, leading to speculation about attempted recentralization at the highest levels.[14] Nonetheless, while

---

[14] A single leader's assuming two top positions is not new: see Hồ Chí Minh following land reform implementation crises (1953–1956) and Trường Chinh in 1986.

postponing review of the Law on Associations, the National Assembly did pass the Law on Access to Information. All these steps suggest a combination of the central state's reasserting control and a move towards more open governance.

Fundamentally, the prospect for one-party political stability in Vietnam will be based on the ability of the VCP, the state, and citizens to institutionalize socialist ideals in a world absent of ideological competition. That Vietnam has been pragmatic and adaptive in practicing Marxism and Leninism is undeniable. If successful, Vietnam, a late developer, will contribute to the history of Leninism in an innovative way. Whichever path the VCP and the government choose, the experience of economic reform that unfolded between 1979 and 1989 has shown that while pressure for change may come from a wide range of sources, successful change has only been brought about by a broad-based, varied coalition of state and non-state sectors.

Vietnam's experience contributes to discussions of regime change and state-building in several respects. It draws attention to "fence-breakers" as drivers of regime change and the decentralized state structure they create. Vietnam's *đổi mới* experience also speaks to the interplay between modern formal rules of law and norms and practices inherited from the old socialist regime as the basis for regime legitimacy and political stability. Finally, state transformation as it evolved during *đổi mới* shows an ongoing process of confrontation and accommodation, both among party-state state elites and between them and the masses, to redefine state structures, authority relations, and public accountability.

List of Acronyms

CMPI	Committee for the Monitoring of Public Investment
DOHA	Department of Home Affairs
DOLISA	Department of Labor, War Invalids, and Social Affairs
DRV	Democratic Republic of Vietnam
ICP	Indochinese Communist Party
INGO	International Non-Governmental Organization
MOHA	Ministry of Home Affairs
MOLISA	Ministry of Labor, War Invalids, and Social Affairs
MPI	Ministry of Planning and Investment
OSS	One-Stop Shop
PAR	Public Administration Reform
PAR-Index	Public Administration Reform Index
PAR-MP	Public Administration Reform Master Program
PIU	People's Inspectorate Unit
SBG	State Business Group
SGC	State General Corporation
SIPAS	Satisfaction Index for Public Administration Services
SOE	State-Owned Enterprise
SRV	Socialist Republic of Vietnam
VCP	Vietnamese Communist Party
VFF	Vietnam Fatherland Front
VNGO	Vietnamese Non-Governmental Organization
VUSTA	Vietnam Union for Science and Technology Associations
WTO	World Trade Organization

References

"Bí thư Tỉnh ủy Kim Ngọc – Một con người đổi mới và sáng tạo" [Party Secretary Kim Ngoc – A Reformist and Innovative Figure], *Nhân Dân Điện Tử* (October 3, 2018).

"Biển miền Trung đã trở lại bình thường sau sự cố Formosa" [Central Vietnam's Coast Returns to Normal after the Formosa Disaster], *Người Lao Động* (May 17, 2018).

"Chuyện 'khoán chui' ở Vĩnh Phúc thời Bí thư Kim Ngọc" [The Story about 'Hidden Sub-Contracting' in Vinh Phuc under Party Secretary Kim Ngoc's Time], *Dân Việt* (September 15, 2017).

"Đầu tư công – thực trạng và giải pháp" [Public Investment: Situation and Solutions], *Kiểm toán Nhà nước Việt Nam* (August 8, 2012).

"Đây là lý do 13 tỉnh thành này, đặc biệt là TPHCM phải 'gánh hộ' ngân sách cho các địa phương còn lại" [These Are Reasons Why 13 Provinces, Especially Ho Chi Minh City, Have to Bear the Budget Burden for the Remaining Provinces!], *CAFEF* (October 14, 2016).

"Dự án Sào Khê đội vốn 36 lần: Đã yêu cầu lãnh đạo tỉnh Ninh Bình báo cáo" [The Sao Khe Project Raised Capital 36 Times: Ninh Binh Leadership Asked to Report the Situation], *Báo Mới* (June 3, 2018).

"Dự án Sào Khê từ 72 tỷ "vọt" lên 2,595 tỷ đồng: Bí thư Tỉnh ủy Ninh Bình nói gì?" [The Sao Khe Project from VND 72 billion to 2,595 billion: What Did Ninh Binh Party Secretary Say?], *VTC News* (May 23, 2018).

"Giảm đầu mối nhưng thực chất lại tăng số Cục, Vụ thuộc Bộ" [Reduced Number of Contact Points, but a Larger Number of Bureaus and Departments within Ministries], *VOV* (August 7, 2017).

"Hành trình tách nhập tỉnh, thành" [Roadmap for the Split and Merger of Provinces and Cities], *Vietnamnet* (September 7, 2017).

"Lại bàn về đầu tư công" [Re-Discuss Public Investment], *Kinh tế Sài Gòn Online* (August 12, 2011).

"Nhiều bộ có số lượng thứ trưởng vượt tiêu chuẩn" [Many Ministries Have More Deputy Ministers Than Standardized], *Báo Đất Việt* (October 17, 2017).

"Nhìn lại việc 'trải thảm đỏ đón nhà đầu tư'" [Reviewing the 'Rolling out the Red Carpet to Welcome Investors' Practice], *Tin tức* (January 31, 2013).

"Thanh tra kết luận nhiều dự án 'đội vốn' ở Hải Phòng" [The Inspectorate Concluded that Many Projects in Hai Phong Had Raised Capital], *VNExpress* (July 17, 2018).

"UBND TP.HCM đã điều chỉnh quy hoạch Thủ Thiêm như thế nào?" [How Did the Ho Chi Minh City People's Committee Adjust the Thu Thiem Project's Spatial Plan?], *Thanh Niên* (May 4, 2018).

"Vietnam Energy Executives Stand Trial on Corruption Charges," *BBC News* (January 8, 2018).

Anderson, Benedict R. O'G. (1983). Old State, New Society: Indonesia's New Order in Comparative Historical Perspective. *Journal of Asian Studies*, 42 (3), 477–96.

Beresford, Melanie & Fforde, Adam (1997). A Methodology for Analysing the Process of Economic Reform in Vietnam: The Case of Domestic Trade. *Journal of Communist Studies and Transition Politics*, 13(4), 99–128.

Beresford, Melanie & Tran Ngoc, Angie, eds. (2004). *Reaching for the Dream: Challenges of Sustainable Development in Vietnam*. Singapore: ISEAS.

Beresford, Melanie (1988). *Vietnam: Politics, Economics and Society*. London and New York: Pinter Publishers.

      (1989). *National Unification and Economic Development in Vietnam*. Houndmills, UK: Palgrave Macmillan.

Bland, Ben. "Vinashin Executives Go on Trial in Vietnam." *Financial Times* (March 27, 2012).

Bộ Nội Vụ (2018). *Báo cáo chỉ số Cải cách Hành chính – PAR Index 2017 [Report on Indicators on Public Administration Reform – PAR Index 2017]*.

Bộ Nội Vụ, Mặt trận Tổ quốc Việt Nam, Hội Cựu chiến binh Việt Nam (2018). *Báo cáo chỉ số hài lòng của người dân, tổ chức đối với sự phục vụ của cơ quan hành chính nhà nước năm 2017 [Report on Indicators on Satisfaction of Citizens and Organizations Regarding the Services of State Management Agencies in 2017 – SIPAS 2017]*.

Bui Tin (1995). *Following Ho Chi Minh: The Memoirs of a North Vietnamese Colonel*. Trans. Judy Stowe and Do Van. Honolulu: University of Hawaii Press.

Chan, Anita & Norlund, Irene (1999). Vietnamese and Chinese Labor Regimes: On the Road to Divergence. In Anita Chan, Benedict J. Tria Kerkvliet, and Jonathan Unger, eds., *Transforming Asian Socialism: China and Vietnam Compared*. Lanham: Rowman & Littlefield Publishers, pp. 204–29.

Châu Hoàng Thân. "Đặc điểm, yêu cầu và thực trạng phân cấp quản lý đất đai hiện nay" [Features, Needs, and Current Situations of Land Management Decentralization]. 26 April 2018. Available at: http://tuphaptamky .gov.vn/2014/news/sua-luat-dat-dai-2013/Dac-diem-yeu-cau-va-thuc-trang-phan-cap-quan-ly-dat-dai-hien-nay-3700.html

Chiến lược ổn định và phát triển kinh tế xã hội đến năm 2000 [Strategy for Socio-Economic Stability and Development to 2000].

Chử Văn Lâm (1990). *45 năm nông nghiệp Việt Nam* [45 Years of Vietnamese Agriculture]. In Viện Kinh tế học, *45 năm kinh tế Việt Nam (1945–1990) [45 Years of the Vietnamese Economy (1945–1990)]*. Hà Nội: Khoa học Xã hội, pp. 94–115.

CODE & PPWG (2008). *Tài liệu hội thảo sự tham gia của tổ chức phi chính phủ và tổ chức cộng đồng trong vận động chính sách: Kinh nghiệm thực tiễn và khuôn khổ pháp luật [Materials on Cooperation]*. Hà Nội: SDC.

CODE (2008). *Vận động chính sách: Thực tiễn và pháp luật [Policy Advocacy: Practice and Laws]*. Hà Nội: Lao Động – Xã hội.

Cương lĩnh xây dựng đất nước trong thời kỳ quá độ lên chủ nghĩa xã hội [Program on the Building of the Country during the Transition to Socialism].

Đảng Cộng sản Việt Nam (2016). *Văn kiện Đại hội Đại biểu toàn quốc lần thứ XII [Documents from the Twelfth National Party Congress]*. Hà Nội: VP Trung ương Đảng.

Đặng Hùng Võ (2012). Phân cấp quyền của Nhà nước đối với đất đai, quản lý đất đai và việc giám sát – đánh giá cần thiết ở Việt Nam [Decentralization of the State Regarding Land, Land Management, and Necessary Monitoring and Supervision in Vietnam]. In *Kỷ yếu Diễn đàn kinh tế mùa Thu năm 2012 [Proceedings from the Fall 2012 Economic Forum]*, Vũng Tàu, September 28–29, 2012.

Dang Phong & Beresford, Melanie (1998). *Authority Relations and Economic Decision-Making in Vietnam: A Historical Perspective*. Copenhagen: NIAS Press.

Đặng Phong (2009a). *"Phá rào" trong kinh tế vào đêm trước đổi mới ["Fence-Breaking" in the Economy the Night before Đổi Mới]*. Hà Nội: Tri thức.

(2009b). *Tư duy kinh tế Việt Nam 1975–1989 (Nhật ký thời bao cấp) [Vietnamese Economic Thinking 1975–1989 (A Memoir from the State Subsidy Era)]*. Hà Nội: Tri thức.

Dapice, David (2008). *Choosing Success: The Lessons of East and Southeast Asia and Vietnam's Future: A Policy Framework for Vietnam's Socioeconomic Development, 2011–2020*. Asia Programs, John. F. Kennedy School of Government, Harvard University.

Davidsen, Søren et al. (2007). *Implementation Assessment of the Anti-Corruption Law: How Far Has Vietnam Come?* Report prepared for the First Anti-Corruption Dialogue, Hanoi, Vietnam.

Đinh Thế Huynh et al. (2015). *30 năm đổi mới và phát triển ở Việt Nam [30 Years of Renewal and Development]*. Hà Nội: Chính trị Quốc gia.

Do Kim Chung, Nguyen Phuong Le, & Luu Van Duy (2015). Implementation of Poverty Reduction Policies: An Analysis of National Targeted Program for Poverty Reduction in the Northwest Region of Vietnam. *International Journal of Business and Social Science*, 9(1), 76–86.

Duiker, William J. (1989). *Vietnam Since the Fall of Saigon (Updated Edition)*. Athens, OH: Ohio University Center for International Studies.

Elliott, David (1992). Vietnam's 1991 Party Elections. *Asian Affairs*, 19(3), 159–69.

Fforde, Adam & Homutova, Lada (2017). Political Authority in Vietnam: Is the VCP a Paper Leviathan? *Journal of Current Southeast Asian Affairs*, 36 (3), 91–118.

Fforde, Adam & Paine, Susanne (1987). *The Limits of National Liberation: Problems of Economic Management in the Democratic Republic of Vietnam*. London: Croom Helm.

Fforde, Adam (2004). *State Owned Enterprises, Law, and a Decade of Market-Oriented Socialist Development in Vietnam*. SEARC Working Paper Series, Hong Kong: City University of Hong Kong.

Fforde, Adam, & de Vylder, Stefan (1996). *From Plan to Market: The Economic Transition in Vietnam*. Boulder, CO: Westview Press.

Fforde, Adam & Goldstone, Anthony (1995). *Vietnam to 2005: Advancing on All Fronts*. London: The Economist Intelligence Unit.

Gainsborough, Martin (2010). *Vietnam: Rethinking the State*. London: Zed Books.

Greenfield, Gerard (1994). The Development of Capitalism in Vietnam. In Ralph Miliband, ed., *Socialist Register* 30, 204–34.

Hansen, Henrik, Rand, John, & Tarp, Finn (2009). Enterprise Growth and Survival in Vietnam: Does Government Support Matter? *The Journal of Development Studies*, 45(7), 1048–69.

Hoàng Văn Hoan (1986). *Giọt nước trong biển cả [Drops of Water in the Ocean]*. Available at: http://lmvn.com/truyen/?func=viewpost&id=diQBlL91SLDT D6TrnXr8pqPRahWde4k9

Houtart, Francois & Lemercinier, Genevieve (1984). *Hai Van: Life in a Vietnamese Commune*. London: Zed Books.

Huy Đức (2012). *Bên thắng cuộc, quyển I và II [The Winning Side, 2 vols.]* Available at: www.vinadia.org/ben-thang-cuoc-huy-duc-quyen-i-giai-phong/; and www.vinadia.org/ben-thang-cuoc-huy-duc-quyen-ii-quyen-binh/

Huynh Kim Khanh (1982). *Vietnamese Communism 1925–1945*. Ithaca: Cornell University Press.

IFC et al. (2011). *Cải cách quy trình và thủ tục hành chính và đầu tư, đất đai và xây dựng [Reform of the Process and Administrative Procedures for Investment, Land, and Construction]*. Hà Nội: Lao Động.

Kahin, George (1986). *Intervention: How America Became Involved in Vietnam*. New York: Alfred A. Knopf.

Kerkvliet, Ben, Heng, Russell, & Koh, David, eds. (2003). *Getting Organized in Vietnam: Moving in and around the Socialist State*. Singapore: ISEAS.

Kerkvliet, Benedict & Marr, David G, eds. (2004). *Beyond Hanoi: Local Government in Vietnam*. Singapore: ISEAS.

Kerkvliet, Benedict (2001). An Approach for Analyzing State-Society Relations in Vietnam. *Sojourn*, 16(2), 238–78.

——— (2014). Government Repression and Toleration of Dissidents in Contemporary Vietnam. In Jonathan London, ed., *Politics in Contemporary Vietnam: Party, State, and Authority Relations*. London: Palgrave Macmillan, pp. 100–34.

Koh, David W. H. (2006). *Wards of Hanoi*. Singapore: ISEAS.

Kornai, Janos (1992). *The Socialist System: The Political Economy of Communism*. Oxford: The Clarendon Press.

Le Duc Thinh & Dao Trung Chinh (2010). *The Crafting of Land Tenure Policies – The Nature and Dynamic of the Actors' Interplay in the Red River Delta*. Report from the Institute of Policy and Strategy for Agriculture and Rural Development, Hanoi.

Le Duc Thinh (2010). *Corruption in Land Administration in Vietnam*. Report from the Institute of Policy and Strategy for Agriculture and Rural Development, Hanoi.

Lê Viết Thái (2012). Phân cấp trong lĩnh vực quy hoạch và kế hoạch ở Việt Nam: Thực trạng và giải pháp [Decentralization in Spatial Planning and Development Planning in Vietnam: Situation and Solutions]. In *Kỷ yếu Diễn đàn kinh tế mùa Thu năm 2012 [Proceedings from the Fall 2012 Economic Forum]*, Vũng Tàu, September 28–29, 2012.

London, Jonathan D., ed. (2011). *Education in Vietnam*. Singapore: ISEAS.

Malesky, E. J. & Taussig. M. (2008). Where Is Credit Due? Legal Institutions, Connections, and the Efficiency of Bank Lending in Vietnam. *Journal of Law, Economics, and Organization*, 25 (June 20), 1–43.

Mody, Ashoka, ed. (1997). *Infrastructure Strategies in East Asia: The Untold Story*. Washington, DC: The World Bank.

Moise, Edwin (1993). *Land Reform in Vietnam and China: Consolidating the Revolution at the Village Level*. Chapel Hill: University of North Carolina Press.

MOLISA & UNDP (2004). *Taking Stock, Planning Ahead: Evaluation of the National Targeted Program on Hunger Eradication and Poverty Reduction and Program 135*. UNDP: Hanoi.

Ngân hàng Thế giới (2012). *Sửa đổi Luật Đất đai để thúc đẩy phát triển bền vững ở Việt Nam* [Revision of the Land Law to Promote Sustainable

Development in Vietnam], Hà Nội: Ngân hàng Thế giới.

Nguyễn Mại (2012). Phân cấp quản lý Kinh tế và FDI [Decentralization of Economic and FDI Management]. In *Kỷ yếu Diễn đàn kinh tế mùa Thu năm 2012 [Proceedings from the Fall 2012 Economic Forum]*, Vũng Tàu, September 28–29, 2012.

Nguyen Thi Thuy (2016). Fiscal Decentralization Trends in Vietnam: Developments and Reforms. *Public Administration and Policy*, 19(2), 31–41.

Paine, Suzy (1988). The Limits of Planning and the Case for Economic Reform. In David Marr and Christian Pelzer White, eds. *Postwar Vietnam: Dilemmas in Socialist Development*. Ithaca, NY: Southeast Asia Program, pp. 91–5.

Phạm Duy Nghĩa (2012). Phân cấp quản lý Nhà nước trong lĩnh vực Kinh tế – Cơ sở lý luận, Thực trạng và Giải pháp [Decentralization of State Management in Economic Areas: Theoretical Basis, Situation, and Solutions]. In *Kỷ yếu Diễn đàn kinh tế mùa Thu năm 2012 [Proceedings from the Fall 2012 Economic Forum]*, Vũng Tàu, September 28–29, 2012.

Phạm Thị Thu Hằng (2014). Một số vấn đề về phát triển khu vực tư nhân [Some Problems in Private Sector Development]. In *Kỷ yếu Diễn đàn kinh tế mùa Thu năm 2014 [Proceedings from the Fall 2014 Economic Forum]*, Ninh Bình, September 27–29, 2014.

Porter, Gareth (1993). *Vietnam: The Politics of Bureaucratic Socialism*. Ithaca, NY: Cornell University.

Riedel, James & Turley, William S. (1999). *The Politics and Economics of Transition to an Open Market Economy in Vietnam*. OECD Development Center, Working Paper no. 152.

SRV Government web portal. http://chinhphu.vn/portal/page/portal/chinhphu/ thanhvienchinhphuquacacthoiky

Tenev, Stoyan et al. (2003). *Informality and the Playing Field in Vietnam's Business Sector*. Washington, DC: World Bank and the International Finance Corporation.

Thayer, Carlyle (2014). The Apparatus of Authoritarian Rule in Vietnam. In Jonathan London, ed., *Politics in Contemporary Vietnam: Party, State, and Authority Relations*. London: Palgrave Macmillan, pp. 135–61.

_____ (1988). The Regularization of Politics: Continuity and Change in the Party's Central Committee 1951–1986. In David G. Marr & Christine P. White, eds., *Postwar Vietnam: Dilemmas in Socialist Development*. Ithaca, NY: Southeast Asia Program, pp. 177–93.

_____ (1994). *The Vietnam People's Army under Doi Moi*. Singapore: ISEAS.

Therborn, Goran (1978). *What Does the Ruling Class Do When It Rules? State Apparatuses and State Power under Feudalism, Capitalism and Socialism.* London: NLB.

Thông báo 1483/TB-TTCP của Thanh tra Chính phủ ngày 4 tháng 9 năm 2018 về kết quả kiểm tra một số nội dung chủ yếu liên quan đến việc khiếu nại của công dân về khu đô thị mới Thủ Thiêm, thành phố Hồ Chí Minh [Government Inspectorate Report 1483/TB-TTCP dated 4 September 2018 on the results of a review of key issues related to citizen petitioning of the Thu Thiem New Urban Area in HCM City].

Trần Du Lịch (2014). Tái Cơ cấu Đầu tư công: Vấn đề và Giải pháp [Restructuring of Public Investment: Problems and Solutions]. In *Kỷ yếu Diễn đàn kinh tế mùa Thu năm 2014 [Proceedings from the Fall 2014 Economic Forum]*, Ninh Binh, September 27–29, 2014.

Trần Tiến Cường (2012). Phân công, phân cấp quản lý doanh nghiệp nhà nước: Thực trạng, nguyên nhân, và một số gợi ý đổi mới [Division of Work and Management Decentralization of SOEs: Situations, Causes, and Suggestions on How to Change]. In *Kỷ yếu Diễn đàn kinh tế mùa Thu năm 2012 [Proceedings from the Fall 2012 Economic Forum]*, Vũng Tàu, September 28–29, 2012.

Truong Chinh (1959). *Resolutely Taking the North Vietnamese Countryside to Socialism through Agricultural Co-Operation.* Hanoi: FLPH.

UNDP (2017). *Poverty Reduction in Vietnam.* UNDP, October 17, 2017.

Van Arkadie, Brian & Mallon, Raymond (2003). *Vietnam: A Transition Tiger?* Canberra: Asia Pacific Press at the Australian National University.

Văn phòng Quốc hội (2016). *Lịch sử Quốc hội Việt Nam, Tập IV (1992–2011) [History of Vietnam's National Assembly, Vol. IV (1992–2011)]*, Hà Nội: Chính trị Quốc gia Sự thật.

Văn Tất Thu (2007). Một số giải pháp kỹ thuật để tổ chức bộ đa ngành đa lĩnh vực [A Number of Technical Solutions for the Organization of Multi-Sectoral and Multi-Functional Ministries]. *Tổ Chức Nhà Nước [State Management]*, (17)12, 24–7.

Vasavakul, Thaveeporn & Bui The Cuong (2008). *Report on the Study on Support for an Official Mechanism for Dialogue between Vietnamese Government Agencies/ the National Assembly and Civil Society Organizations in Vietnam*, A Report Prepared for the SDC, Hanoi.

Vasavakul, Thaveeporn & Nguyen Thai Van (2006). *Collaboration Groups in Rural Vietnam: A Background Paper.* A Report Prepared for Oxfam-Vietnam.

Vasavakul, Thaveeporn (1995). Vietnam: The Changing Model of Political Legitimation. In Muthiah Alagappa, ed., *Political Legitimacy in Southeast Asia.* Stanford: Stanford University Press, pp. 257–87.

(1996). Politics of Administrative Reform in Post-Socialist Vietnam. In Suiwah Leung, ed., *Vietnam Assessment: Creating a Sound Investment Climate.* Singapore: ISEAS, pp. 42–68.

(1997). Sectoral Politics and Strategies for State and Party Building from the VII to the VIII Congress of the Vietnamese Communist Party (1991–1996). In Adam Fforde, ed., *Doi Moi: Ten Years after the 1986 Party Congress.* Canberra: Department of Political and Social Change Monograph Series no. 24, pp. 81–135.

(1999). Rethinking the Philosophy of Central-Local Relations in Post-Central Planning Vietnam. In Mark Turner, ed., *Central-Local Government Relations in the Asia-Pacific Region.* London: Macmillan, pp. 166–95.

(1999a). Vietnam: Sectors, Classes, and the Transformation of a Leninist State. In James W. Morley, ed., *Driven by Growth: Political Change in the Asia-Pacific Region* (revised edition). Armonk, NY: M.E. Sharpe, pp. 58–82.

(2000). Ý thức dân tộc Việt Nam trong cách nhìn so sánh [Vietnamese Nationalism from a Comparative Perspective]. In *Việt Nam học: Kỷ yếu Hội thảo Quốc tế lần thứ nhất, Hà Nội, 15–17/7/1998.* Hà Nội: Thế Giới, pp. 400–8.

(2002). *Rebuilding Authority Relations: Public Administration Reform in the Era of Doi Moi.* A Report Prepared for the Asian Development Bank, Hanoi.

(2003a). From Fence Breaking to Networking: Popular Organisations and Policy Influence in Post-Socialist Vietnam. In Benedict Kerkvliet, Russell Heng and David Koh, eds., *Getting Organised in Vietnam: Moving in and Around the Socialist State.* Singapore: ISEAS, pp. 25–61.

(2003b). *Mapping Vietnam's Legal Cultures: Reflections on Corruption, Organized Crime, and State Building in the Post-Socialist Era.* Paper presented at the "Vietnam Legal Culture Symposium," University of Victoria, Canada from March 27–29, 2003.

(2006). Public Administration Reform and Practices of Co-Governance: Towards a Change in Governance and Governance Cultures in Vietnam. In Heinrich Böll Foundation, ed., *Active Citizens under Political Wraps: Experiences from Myanmar/Burma and Vietnam.* Chiang Mai: Santipab Pack Print, pp. 143–65.

(2008). *Recrafting State Identity: Corruption and Anti-Corruption in Doi Moi Vietnam from a Comparative Perspective.* Paper prepared for the workshop "Remaking the State," organized by Jonathan London, City University of Hong Kong, August 21–22, 2008.

(2012). *Governance Arrangements in Vietnam's Provinces: Pathways toward Inclusive Growth and Poverty Reduction*. A Report Prepared for the Embassy of Norway, Hanoi.

(2013). Beyond the Vietnam War: Vietnamese Socialism Today. In Shannon Brincat, ed. *Communism in the 21st Century: Whither Communism (Vol. 2)*. Santa Barbara, CA: Praeger, pp. 135–59.

(2014). Authoritarianism Reconfigured: Evolving Accountability Relations within Vietnam's One-Party Rule. In Jonathan London, ed., *Politics in Contemporary Vietnam: Party, State, and Authority Relations*. London: Palgrave Macmillan UK, pp. 42–63.

Vasavakul, Thaveeporn et al. (2009a). *Analysis of Vietnam's Current Legal Framework on People's Councils: A Perspective from Ninh Thuan*. A Report Prepared for Oxfam-Vietnam.

Vasavakul, Thaveeporn, Le Viet Thai, & Le Thi Phi Van (2009). *Public Administration and Economic Development in Vietnam: Remaking the Public Administration for the 21st Century*, UNDP's Public Administration Reform and Anti-Corruption: A Series of Policy Discussion Papers.

Vickerman, Andrew (1986). *The Fate of the Peasantry: Premature Transition to Socialism in the Democratic Republic of Vietnam*. New Haven: Yale Southeast Asian Studies Monographs Series 24.

Vietnam Executive Leadership Program (2012). *Structural Reform for Growth, Equity, and National Sovereignty*. Asia Programs, John F. Kennedy School of Government.

(2013). *Unplugging Institutional Bottlenecks to Restore Growth*. Asia Programs, John F. Kennedy School of Government.

(2015). *Institutional Reform: From Vision to Reality*. A Policy Discussion Paper Prepared for the Vietnam Executive Leadership Program, Harvard Kennedy School.

Vũ Sỹ Cường (2012). Phân cấp quản lý Ngân sách nhà nước ở Việt Nam và định hướng Đổi Mới [Decentralization of the State Budget Management in Vietnam and Directions for Change]. In *Kỷ yếu Diễn đàn kinh tế mùa Thu năm 2012 [Proceedings from the Fall 2012 Economic Forum]*, Vũng Tàu, September 28–29, 2012.

Vũ Sỹ Cường et al. (2014). Cơ chế phân bố vốn đầu tư nhà nước: Thực trạng và giải pháp thể chế [Mechanisms in Allocating Investment Capital: Situations and Institutional Solutions]. In *Kỷ yếu Diễn đàn kinh tế mùa Thu năm 2014 [Proceedings from the Fall 2014 Economic Forum]*, Ninh Bình, September 27–29, 2014.

Vu Thanh Tu Anh (2016). Vietnam Decentralization amidst Fragmentation. *Journal of Southeast Asian Economies*, 33(2), 188–208.

Vu Thanh Tu Anh (2017). Does WTO Accession Help Domestic Reform?: The Political Economy of SOE Reform Backsliding in Vietnam. *World Trade Review*, 16(1), 85–109.

Vu Thanh Tu Anh, Le Viet Thai, Vo Tat Thang (2007). *Provincial Extra-legal Investment Incentives in the Context of Decentralisation in Vietnam: Mutually Beneficial or a Race to the Bottom?* Hanoi: UNDP.

Wells-Dang, Andrew (2012). *Civil Society Networks in China and Vietnam: Informal Pathbreakers in Health and the Environment*. Houndmills, UK: Palgrave Macmillan.

Werner, Jayne (1988). "The Problem of District in Vietnam's Development Policy." In David Marr and Christian Pelzer White, eds. *Postwar Vietnam: Dilemmas in Socialist Development*. Ithaca, NY: Southeast Asia Program, pp. 147–62.

White, Christine (1981). *Agrarian Reform and National Liberation in the Vietnamese Revolution: 1920–1957*. Ph.D. dissertation. Ithaca, NY: Cornell University.

(1985). Agricultural Planning, Pricing Policy, and Co-operatives in Vietnam. *World Development*, 13(1), 97–114.

World Bank (2008). *Vietnam Development Report 2009: Capital Matters*. Washington, DC: World Bank.

Acknowledgments

The author thanks Edward Aspinall, Adam Fforde, Meredith Weiss, three anonymous reviewers, and three nonspecialist readers for their comments on early drafts. The author is responsible for any remaining shortcomings in this Element.

Politics and Society in Southeast Asia

Edward Aspinall
Australian National University

Edward Aspinall is a professor of politics at the Coral Bell School of Asia-Pacific Affairs, Australian National University. A specialist of Southeast Asia, especially Indonesia, much of his research has focused on democratisation, ethnic politics and civil society in Indonesia and, most recently, clientelism across Southeast Asia.

Meredith L. Weiss
University at Albany, SUNY

Meredith L. Weiss is Professor of Political Science at the University at Albany, SUNY. Her research addresses political mobilization and contention, the politics of identity and development, and electoral politics in Southeast Asia, with particular focus on Malaysia and Singapore.

About the Series

The Elements series Politics and Society in Southeast Asia includes both country-specific and thematic studies on one of the world's most dynamic regions. Each title, written by a leading scholar of that country or theme, combines a succinct, comprehensive, up-to-date overview of debates in the scholarly literature with original analysis and a clear argument.

Cambridge Elements ≡

Politics and Society in Southeast Asia

Printed in the United States
By Bookmasters